accolades

"This is *the* book for single women sizing up a man. Debra Weiner has written an encyclopedia all about decoding male behavior. She explains how to recognize trouble, interpret it, and run! It is wonderfully written, wise, and enlightening. You should not leave your single state without it!"
—Margo Howard, "Dear Margo" for Creators Syndicate and www.wowowow.com

"Single women everywhere, listen up! Do not leave for a date without slipping your lipstick and Debra Weiner's *How to Recognize Your Future Ex-Husband* into your bag. It's a veritable dating bible, and I wish I'd had her settle-or-else advice in my pocket 60 dates ago. Weiner deftly dissects dysfunctional men and their relationship patterns with clear and certain language, and tells you exactly when it's appropriate to run for the hills. She demonstrates how to recognize when you just shouldn't be that into him and why. Her style is frank, honest and free of cliches—exactly how a book about dating and finding the perfect mate should be."
—Rachel Machacek, author of *The Science of Single: One Woman's Grand Experiment in Modern Dating, Creating Chemistry, and Finding Love*

"One read of Debra Weiner's *How to Recognize Your Future Ex-Husband*, will have you leap over an 'ex,' and head straight for a prince! A fun and straight-forward format offers sound advice that makes great sense."
—Laurie Graff, author of *You Have to Kiss a Lot of Frogs* and *The Shiksa Syndrome*

"With her warm and engaging prose, Debra Weiner shares personal experiences and thought-provoking commentaries that will help readers to steer clear of that wishy-washy path to Mr. Wrong. Even married couples will benefit by becoming aware of their own potentially-alienating behaviors!"

—Kristin Espinasse, author of *Words in a French Life*

"Debra is wise, witty, and perceptive, with an unerring b.s. detector. Where was she when I was deciding who to marry, and (disastrously) what to let slide? Let this book be your eyes when you find yourself blinded by love."

—Candace Walsh, editor, *Ask Me About My Divorce: Women Open Up About Moving On*

"*How to Recognize Your Future Ex-Husband* is a girl's go-to guide for choosing healthy, lasting relationships. With wit and wisdom, Debra Weiner provides a treasure chest of strategies for finding Mr. Right—without losing yourself. A must-read for women of all ages."

—Irene Vitale, founder and editor, www.girlsTalk.com

"Debra Weiner's book will help even the savviest of daters. Get ready to have your eyes opened."

—Margot Leitman, Comedian, Actress, Writer

how to recognize your future ex-husband

how to recognize your future ex-husband

a guide for successful mating *by* **Debra Weiner**

Copyright © 2011 by Debra Weiner

All rights reserved. No part of this book may be reproduced, stored in a retrieval system, or transmitted in any form or by any means, electronic, mechanical, photocopying, recording or otherwise, without the prior permission in writing by Debra Weiner.

Published in the United States by Fossanova.

ISBN: 978-0-578-05868-9

Printed in the United States of America

Book Design by Darryl Fossa

First Edition

contents

acknowledgements	v	humor	61
foreword	vii	internet dating	63
the arthur files	ix	interrogation	66
questions, answers & etcs	xiii	jealousy	69
addiction	1	lateness	72
age difference	4	lying	74
anger	7	manners	76
boundaries	10	married men	78
children	16	money	82
commitment phobia	20	narcissism	86
conflict avoidance	24	passive-aggressive behavior	89
control	27	past relationships	91
conversation	30	pornography	94
core needs	34	rationalization	97
criticism	37	religion	103
cursing	40	safety	106
dependency	42	sex	108
family relationships	47	soul-mate-at-first-sight phenomenon	112
fit	53	trust	117
helplessness	57	asking questions we are afraid to ask	121

For Susan Lanir, whose wisdom and insight changed my life and inspired this book.

acknowledgements

I would like to thank the following people for their contribution to the overall Gestalt: Jack Dickerson, Susan Lanir, and Sari Kramer for facilitating successful transference; Paul Brala for introducing the notion of boundaries; Pierino Cipolloni for his well-timed incantations; Carol Posthumous and Holly Caster for editorial support; Darryl Fossa for love and tolerance; Jeffrey Tarnoff for co-piloting the plane; and Jed Waldman for being the über-est of friends.

foreword

The idea for this book came about during a conversation I had with one of my former therapists when we were talking about how prevalent the rationalization process was among women we knew. This led to her sharing a story with me about a friend of hers who had recently called to tell her all about a new relationship and how she had found "the one." After politely listening to her friend speak almost exclusively in superlatives (based on four weeks of dating), she said, "Congratulations. I think you have just met your future ex-husband." I was so enthralled by the phrase that I began to work on a project that would evolve into this book.

I have had the good fortune of spending many years working with gifted therapists who have helped me gain a better understanding of some of the more questionable choices I have made in my life. Much of that time was spent addressing the difficulties I encountered in my romantic relationships. The pattern, up until my marriage almost ten years ago, was to be attracted to emotionally unavailable men. Often times brilliant——but broken——people who could not get out of their own way. What gave these relationships more longevity than was appropriate was my ability to rationalize everything that did not intuitively feel right. In my desire for connection and meaning, I suspended my values and darkened the lights so I would not be able to see what was wrong with the picture.

How to Recognize Your Future Ex-Husband has been written to help you navigate through the dating process in your quest to find a mate and alert you to "the signals from within" that we often ignore. It addresses the most common questions, dilemmas, and doubts that emerge in the earliest stages of getting to know another person in the first few weeks and months of dating. While it has been written for women, everything that is discussed can and does apply to both sexes. If you are a happily married person browsing through this book, know that these same issues springing up in the context of a long-standing marriage require a different lens for examination.

The topics, questions, and answers are an amalgamation of the hundreds of questions that I have asked, and the clarifying answers that I have received discussing everything from addiction, anger, boundaries, money, passive-aggressive behavior to the soul-mate-at-first-sight phenomenon——given in alphabetical order. Rather than an expert commentary on relationships, these are simply the recipes that I have uncovered and tested many times in my own kitchen. There are many ways to approach relationships, and this is by no means meant to contradict or eclipse all of the other ways to approach the mating process. The remarks that accompany the questions and answers are my personal vignettes that are meant to further illustrate the "recognition" challenges we encounter over the course of our relationships. One of my all-time favorite self-help books is *How to Be Your Own Best Friend* by Mildred Newman and Bernard Berkowitz. This book was organized to emulate its simple and straightforward style.

I hope that *How to Recognize Your Future Ex-Husband* will encourage you to trust your intuition, dismantle your favorite rationalizations, and help you to distinguish which doubts may be discarded and which ones must be listened to in your quest for lasting partnership.

the arthur files

Many years ago I met a man with whom I was completely captivated.

Arthur was funny, smart, and lethally sarcastic. We connected fairly quickly and he eventually moved his life from a Washington DC suburb to create a new life with me in the New York City metro area. He was a physician by training and a freelance medical writer by choice, and earned a very handsome living, most of which he wasn't claiming on his tax returns so he had even more than he would have had otherwise. Because of his positive cash flow, most of our time before he moved was spent in expensive bed & breakfasts, quaint hotels in New Orleans' French Quarter, eating out at fairly high-end restaurants, and flying between DC and New York to visit each other on alternate weekends.

When he came to New York, we often stayed at his favorite Manhattan hotel. He didn't like sleeping at my place, which was a house I shared with a close friend in northern New Jersey. On one of the rare occasions when he did visit, he was appalled that another close friend "dropped by" without calling. In his world, people didn't drop by, namely because there weren't very many people in his world. He had a colorful and troubled history. The child of Orthodox Jewish Hungarian immigrants, he grew up in Brooklyn's Borough Park section. Imagine what would have happened if the stork had dropped off Orson Welles on a Flatbush Avenue stoop instead of a middle-class Milwaukee suburb. Here was someone whose life would have flourished if he had grown up on the Upper West Side of Manhattan and went to a public school instead of a yeshiva.

It wasn't until medical school that he experienced any significant relating with women. As one could guess, his delayed sexual awakening exploded into an all-or-nothing situation. He fell in love with a medical school classmate who had red hair and Italian parents. The timing of this was unfortunate because it coincided with his being accepted into a highly prestigious radiology residency. She was headed elsewhere, so he dropped out of the residency and they soon married. The marriage did not last, and he had what could politely be called a nervous breakdown, which lasted long enough to personally and professionally derail him for quite some time. He never went back to complete his residency, had a few jobs here and there, and then discovered the world of freelance medical writing. This is how we met. He was invited to speak at the medical communications company I was working for to provide an overview on current treatments for epilepsy.

We hit it off immediately. At the time, I still had a compulsive attraction to sarcastic, emotionally unavailable men, and he was able to deliver more densely caloric barbs than anyone I knew. He was what you would get if you crossed Gore Vidal with Zero Mostel. Can you spell "irresistible"?

So I had all of this information: repressed Orthodox Jewish upbringing, parents who were unhappily married, contempt for his mother, disgust for his father, affection for his grandparents, pity for his sister, and derision for everyone else. Of course, he saved the most hostile feelings for himself. He once told me, "I hate people, but you're not people." I was foolish enough to think that this conferred protection from inclement relationship weather. It didn't. In fact, it had the reverse affect. We could not stay together because he *could* talk to me, because I *got* him. I understood him, and knew his back pages. It was simply too much. His wounds had been exposed and he was going to forcibly sew them up before they could naturally heal.

Because of how close we were in nature, it was hard to imagine how he could be okay with knowing that we would never go to the New York Film

Festival or travel through Europe, and all of the other interesting things we had planned to do together. But the real ouch was trying to understand how he could so blithely accept the immediate consequence of breaking up: not speaking to me every day. This was the truly magical part of our connection——the talking. He was very funny, a great storyteller, and we never ran out of things to talk about. This was a bitter lesson in seeing how different people are, how we do not all share the same needs or, if we do, not everyone gives themselves permission to have those needs filled. In sum, we cannot "love someone out" of their own self-loathing.

It took me several years to get past this profound disappointment, and I can honestly say that I wouldn't have been able to move on if a close friend hadn't lived with me for the two to three years immediately following the breakup. He provided friendship, laughter, support, and endless hours of listening and very meaningful feedback.

It was this friend who distracted me enough from my pain so I could see things more clearly. His lacerating, spot-on humor was the key to my reclamation. I had once complained to him that while living with Arthur, I had been dismayed to discover his beard trimmings in the bathroom sink. Bathrooms make me sort of queasy to begin with, and seeing this really put me over the top. So one day I came home after work to see this construct on the kitchen counter: an 8 ½" x 11" piece of cardboard with a tuft of shaving cream, hair, soap scum, and God knows what else. I almost hurled, and then remembered what this was vis-à-vis my ex. One of many creative "interventions" that my friend had staged during my recovery from Arthur.

Why did it take me so long to grieve? Why was I even grieving? I did not have an answer to this until very recently. Now, I believe that my lingering sadness had everything to do with how much I identified with the not-so-healthy parts of Arthur's personality. I couldn't distinguish what was him and what was me, and what used to be me but wasn't who I was anymore. I remember someone telling me at the time that his breaking up with me was a great thing, because it would create a space for the right person to walk in to my life. Which is of course exactly what happened.

questions
answers
&
etcs

addiction

So many people today are in 12-step programs and others struggle and never find their way to recovery. Is it possible to have a successful relationship with someone who has addiction issues or is it doomed from the start?

It depends on the stage of recovery and the people involved. The most important thing to understand is that if you are dating an active addict of any kind, they are not having a relationship with you——they are having a relationship with their addiction. There are hundreds of books that you can read about addiction and we don't need to go into the complex details here. However, one of the foundational ground rules of any 12-step program is that addicts must remove themselves from everyone that they were involved with when they were active. This doesn't mean that people get divorced upon entering the program, but it does mean that they take a hard look at who they have been spending time with and decide if these people do or do not contribute to their sobriety.

It is safe to say that most romantic relationships that involve addiction are codependent. Meaning there is one person who is addicted to the substance and the other person is addicted to the addict. Usually it is very difficult to migrate out of that process because there has been so much unhealthy fusing and insufficiently established boundaries.

Dating someone who is in the initial stages of recovery can be challenging. Sex and romance can be dangerous triggers for addicts and can substantially threaten the early stages of their sobriety. If you are dating someone who has been sober for a number of years, then the rules are different and you would deal with them in much the same way that you would with any other person. In some cases, a recovering addict has more potential for being present and grappling with things in a mature and balanced manner because he has gone through such a thorough examination of his own issues.

A very long time ago I was involved in a relationship that began in college with someone who had a lot of issues. Two of them were smoking marijuana and drinking, in that order. Despite being very intelligent, David became very dependent on marijuana in college and this caused a lot of problems academically and socially. I fell into the classic codependent pattern: as he became more addicted to alcohol and marijuana, I became more addicted to him.

It wasn't until many years later that a very dear friend (and therapist) basically told me that this vicious cycle would never stop until I resolved to no longer speak to him or see him until he got help. So one day, after the umpteenth time he called me to tell me how depressed he was and how sorry he felt about all of the abusive things that had occurred in our relationship, I said, "David, you are no longer allowed to contact me until you get help. You cannot go on binges, call me afterwards for catharsis, and then resume bingeing. I am removing myself from you as of this conversation." I did what you are supposed to do with active addicts——fire them. A week later he made an appointment with a therapist who made him call Alcoholics Anonymous while he was in her office. She insisted that he write down all of the meeting days, times, and locations and promise that he would go to 90 meetings in 90 days. This was the beginning of his recovery, which I believe is now in its 25th year. It was also the beginning of my recovery and understanding that it is impossible to have a relationship with an active addict.

If you have met someone who exhibits any sort of compulsive behavior and is hapless and always in some sort of quandary, save yourself first and move on. It will never work. Ever.

age difference

When I was growing up it was much more common to see an older man and a younger woman together. Today, it has become almost chic for women to date much younger men, and they are referred to by the media as "cougars." If two people love each other and get along reasonably well, how important is age in relation to lasting attraction and happiness?

It all depends on who you are and who he is——and the support systems that you both have in place. I am aware of many successful relationships where there has been a rather large difference in the ages of the people involved. In these cases there was a lot going on that bridged the gap, such as shared interests, which cannot be overlooked. If a 25-year-old woman meets a 50-year-old man and they both share a passion for art or music, then that can be a big tube of glue.

Alongside that there need to be shared values and a similar map of the world, as would be required in any potential partnership. If the woman is looking for security and the man is looking for vitality, then that is something that can hold it together for a good stretch of time. Where it can come apart is when the younger woman decides she might want some more vitality as the older man eventually settles in to the more mundane aspects of the relationship, and doesn't require the same level of stimulation.

One of the best examples of how this situation can play out is seen in the movie *Hannah and Her Sisters*, where Barbara Hershey plays Hannah's sister Lee, who has been involved with a much older, very intense artist named Frederick, played by Max Von Sydow. It has been a teacher/student relationship for quite some time, but things shift when Lee tires of being the student and wants more mutuality. There is always a danger of that, along with what the aging process imposes on us. A 40-year-old woman will most likely not have the same health issues as a 60-year-old man, and I have known some women who have felt very oppressed by having to deal with that reality.

One woman in particular is going through a rough time. She wants to go out dancing on the weekends and her husband wants to stay home and play computer chess. When they first got together they both enjoyed going to clubs and having a very active social life. Over time his pace has slowed and hers has not. As a result there is a large hole in the relationship that she is seeking to fill outside of it. She has indulged in some rather extensive flirtations with men who have similar interests. This is clearly a threat to the relationship but may continue, due to her need for a specific kind of companionship. Now, the security is playing second fiddle to her desire for stimulation. This is a big consideration when pondering a future with someone who is much older.

If you are Madonna, Mary Tyler Moore, or Susan Sarandon, age difference may be of no consequence, but for most of us it is, and definitely deserves an honest look into your motivation and your need for this type of relationship. I have my doubts as to a 35-year-old man easily accepting the enormous effects of menopause on a relationship. It is difficult to imagine Brad Pitt leaving Angelina Jolie and finding eternal bliss with Helen Mirren, despite her obvious appeal. Yet it isn't difficult to imagine Lindsay Lohan falling in love with Brad Pitt!

While I always dated men who were my age, I ended up marrying someone who is five years younger, though it is something that neither of us ever thinks about now.

I have some friends who have older partners, but for the most part they have so much in common that the age difference is unnoticeable. I have other friends with younger partners where I can see how the age difference has strained the relationship. When I was much younger, I was fascinated by the May-December kind of romance and had read about famous couples such as Sophia Loren and Carlo Ponti. Now we have Calista Flockhart and Harrison Ford who seem to have a vital and loving relationship. Perhaps that is how it will remain, but who can say what the next ten years will bring?

I can't imagine myself ever being attracted to a much younger man. I think it would play out like the classic Steely Dan song "Hey Nineteen," and there just wouldn't be much to talk about after awhile.

anger

I have dated men who are angry a great deal of the time, and I have not always understood why. Anger bothers me, but I also know that expressing anger is a healthy thing. Is this my problem or theirs?

Anger is part of our survival pack. Anger creates boundaries, like emotional fences. When a lion roars, we don't want to get closer and pet it. In certain situations, creating boundaries is important, but when somebody is overly angry it implies unresolved hurt. We use anger as a way of feeling less hurt and less vulnerable. If you notice that a person is frequently angry or overly angry, that is an alert for emotional instability. You've heard about rage-aholics? They really are addicted to rage as a first-line response, and it's not only destructive, but also dangerous. Overly angry behavior often suggests somebody who is vulnerable and fragile, somebody who has to create artificial power——anger——to protect himself.

That is a true danger sign, especially if the anger doesn't fit the context of what's happening.

You must not deny the impact that his anger has on you!

It might be important to examine whether you had a very angry father. We all have our parents' relationship imprinted on us from the time we are born. You might be drawn to an angry boyfriend because it's a familiar pattern. It is important to be able to evaluate if his anger is valid, and worthy of being related to in some way.

However, it is of utmost importance for the two of you to talk about discriminating between anger that is a result of something that has happened, or anger that is a result of your boyfriend just being an angry person. Overly angry people are in a perpetual power struggle with other people and that is the first sign of likely "ex-ness."

People who fly into a rage always make a bad landing.
——Will Rogers

I have an uncomfortable relationship to anger. It's not easy for me to articulate my feelings at the moment I am feeling angry. I tend to deflect it, bury it, or hurl it back when it's unexpectedly triggered by something completely unrelated. Because I grew up with a rage-filled father, I am both repelled and attracted to anger. I am put off when others are angry, but for me, expressing it can feel cathartic and clarifying.

In one of my earlier "starter" relationships——with the aforementioned David in the "Addiction" discussion——we were what can only be described as a junior version of George and Martha in *Who's Afraid of Virginia Woolf.* Anger was its strongest aroma, and it was also a bonding agent. Because he was emotionally unavailable most of the time, and became even more so once he started using drugs and alcohol, fighting was the most immediate means I had to make contact. It was familiar to me because I grew up with a hot-tempered father who had a very short fuse and I became accustomed to a pattern of him screaming and cursing at me. That would be followed not by an overt apology, but by some unsolicited act of generosity (like a new coat or new book). Arguing was a way to gain my father's undivided attention, and I used this later in life when involved with another narcissistically damaged person. I didn't realize then the purpose that the anger served: protection from any real intimacy.

As women, we have been socialized to dampen and hold in our anger. In movies, the big strong man sees his woman writhing with repressed anger and he says "she's so cute when she's angry." If our anger is not taken seriously, we may end up withholding it, and it will accumulate until we explode. Or it will stay repressed and make us unhappy and even sick. A friend recalled being pleasantly surprised and enlightened when an angry outburst of hers about some societal injustice elicited her date's admiring reply, "I love a woman with balls!"

Women are validly afraid that showing anger might be viewed as negative, as their comfortable stereotype is to be good, kind, loving, and motherly. So it's important to find someone who will not be threatened by your appropriately expressed anger.

boundaries

Several years ago, a friend of mine met a woman at a music festival. By day three they had already slept together and were talking about saving their oyster shells for their grandchildren. When I told this story to another friend, who is also a therapist, his response was that they didn't have good boundaries. What does that mean? Isn't it possible to have a romantic beginning like that and have it not be something unhealthy? Isn't it the suspension of boundaries that allows for romance in the first place?

With respect to this particular story, I would probably agree with your therapist friend, and say that there was an inappropriate sense of urgency about getting together so quickly and "futurizing" about the oyster shells.

In simple terms, boundaries are something that separates us from everyone else. They are like emotional fences——holding something in and keeping something out. They allow us to survive outside of the pouch, so to speak. How do you feel when other people create boundaries? When someone says "Please stop doing that" or "I don't think I like how you are speaking to me" and it makes you feel anxious and uncomfortable, then you probably have issues with personal boundaries. In the best of all worlds we are taught as young children that we have a right to a certain amount of emotional and physical space, a "no-fly zone" that others must respect. In turn, we learn that other people appreciate the same air traffic rules and we need to act in accordance with that awareness. If you grew up in a family where people's feelings or bodies weren't respected, then your boundaries will most likely be extreme in one direction or the other. You will either have a tall fence or no fence at all.

I'm not sure I get the fence analogy. Why is it all or nothing?

It doesn't have to be, but when you struggle with boundaries that is what it typically looks like until you've moved somewhere toward the middle, where there's a fence, but not one that blocks everyone's view. I am sure that you have seen people with overstated boundaries. I was once on the subway and I remember standing up, holding onto the pole in the middle, squished in along with everyone else on the E train going to work. The train stopped suddenly and lurched, and this woman next to me said, "Can you please move over? Your arm is touching me." I was flabbergasted, because there wasn't any room to move and it was just an inappropriate thing to say in that type of situation. She would be someone who has a high fence. The other side of that is someone I know who was sitting on a bus on the way home from work. She was sitting in the aisle seat reading the paper, which was fanned open like a tent surrounding her. All of a sudden the man sitting in the window seat put his hand on her thigh. She was startled and distressed but didn't say anything. She waited until the bus arrived at her stop and then she got up and said, "Hey, get your hands off of me!" That is someone with a fence that's way too low. If she had left the bus without saying anything, she would be someone with no fence at all.

Why didn't she jump up and scream when she first felt his hand on her thigh?

My guess would be that it terrified her——but somewhere she had been taught that it wasn't okay to put her own feelings of discomfort first. She probably didn't want to embarrass the man or call attention to herself. The key here is that when threatened, she didn't respond appropriately. She was accommodating instead of being self-protective and maintaining her boundaries.

How do you develop boundaries if they don't come naturally to you?

Practice, like everything else. You start small. When someone asks you if you are too cold or too hot, tell them the truth instead of saying "I'm fine" and remaining physically uncomfortable. When a friend calls and asks you to go to the movies and you'd rather stay home, say so, even if you have to fake a chore or an upset stomach if you want to avoid an outright insult to your friend. Take a small risk that speaking up for what you want will be accepted and not feel threatening to the other person. Of course in some cases it can, but you can't allow that possibility to redirect your preferences on a daily basis. The worst that will happen is that the person will express disappointment or try to negotiate, both of which are very acceptable responses to which you can respond, without malice.

How can you tell on the first few dates if a man has bad boundaries, besides his wanting to get physical too quickly?

When he asks a question like, "Will the children have your nose or mine?" that's a clear indication that you've met your future ex-husband.

I grew up in a family where boundaries were either overstated or nonexistent, and it was often very confusing knowing what the "appropriate" response was to very mundane things. One evening when I was 14 years old, I was up late at night watching TV. I got hungry and went to the refrigerator and saw that there was a pickle——one pickle——left in the jar, and I ate it. The next day I heard my father screaming for me to come into the kitchen. He was ranting and raving saying, "Don't you EVER eat the last pickle left in the jar! This isn't your house and you are not the boss——I am !" It was certainly an over-the-top example of his view of boundaries. It was episodes like this that conditioned me to have certain responses to things. So I spent the next 30 years either feeling entitled and self-righteous about taking a pickle that wasn't mine, or guilty and undeserving for wanting it in the first place. Context is everything.

Oh, and in case you are wondering, the friends with the oysters are now divorced. Unfortunately, the initial luminescence did not predict or help sustain them as they encountered the subsequent challenges of marriage, career, and parenthood.

children

For many women it is important to marry a man who wants children, and who is very clear about it from the beginning. What happens if you date someone you really like, who seems like "a fit" but he expresses doubts about wanting children. Is this a bad omen? Aren't we all a bit ambivalent about having kids until we are in a situation where it makes sense to have a family? Isn't it possible that someone can change his mind?

If somebody says he might not want children, it is of the utmost importance to believe him and talk about what the difficulties are. You need for him to clarify his statement. Is he scared? If so, I would ask him, "What do you imagine it would be like for you if you had children?" The way to deal with any fear is to get it out, discuss the nature of it, and explore it as deeply and honestly as possible. But don't pretend you didn't hear it or that he didn't mean it. It's a flashing red light of an issue that needs to be discussed and looked at from all angles. Do not tell yourself that he will change! Do not tell yourself that when he sees a baby he will love it. For women, it's so easy to imagine a man being thrilled at the thought of a baby. Sometimes it's true, but if it isn't, here begins the road toward resentment and eventually anger, rage, and hurt.

What if you are dating someone who has children and you are not comfortable with how he manages them. Is it okay to say something?

Of course it's fine to say something. In a relationship there cannot be issues that are too sacred to be talked about. If there are, that's a form of repression and that, in itself, is a portent of derailment. Having said that, it's important to be clear with yourself about what's bothering you. What is the nature of what you don't like about how he treats his children? The first question to ask yourself is, "Is he treating his children the way I was treated by my parents?" You have to be open to the idea of differences——nobody holds a patent on child-rearing techniques. And although modern psychology has begun to write the first paragraph on how to care for children, the information is constantly changing. You need to be clear on whether there's enough room between the two of you to have differences, even if his way of dealing with children is different from how you'd do it. If you see things, however, that are abusive, disrespectful, and/or violent, run as fast as you can. And appeal to your priest, pastor, or rabbi for the child's sake, or notify the child protection authorities.

When I was a child, I was always suspicious of couples who didn't have children. Perhaps I felt it was a sign that they wouldn't like *me*. In any case, I started naming my children as early as I can remember——assigning names and family relationships to my Barbie® and baby dolls. I couldn't imagine not having children then. Alas, as it turns out, I have never had children of my own. I married later in life and have had the privilege of being one of four parents to a wonderful daughter. She was ten years old when we first met, and to my credit (and years of prior therapy), I did not make the mistake of wanting to be her mommy. Instead, I treated her like I would any new friend, but was very conscious of making sure that she was comfortable, always had food in the house that she would like, and soon converted my home office into a bedroom for her so she would have her own personal space when she visited. If I were younger and dating now, the question of children would be important, and I hope that I would believe someone if he told me he didn't want them.

If you are dating someone who has children, it is important to pay attention to how he is managing them. Is there a lot of sulking and tantrums and an inability to control the child? If so, pay attention, because that could be an important indication that he has boundary issues, which will certainly surface very quickly in your relationship. Just as parents can give you a lot of information about the origins of their children's behavior, children can give you a good peek into their parents' struggles in an overt way.

commitment phobia

I've been dating a man for six months. We see each other every weekend, and speak almost daily on the phone. The other day, I was at his apartment, and I heard him listening to a voicemail message on the speaker phone from another woman. This made me feel insecure, and I asked him if we had an exclusive relationship. He hesitated, and said he wasn't sure. I know he has had many other relationships, which for whatever reason never led to living together or marriage. I really like him, but I don't want to fall into my pattern of giving someone enough "space" so that he will want to be with me exclusively. What are the real chances of him not being so tentative after a certain period of time has gone by?

I hear the sob in your throat as you pose this question. Leave now and avoid heartbreak, which is what you're going to have. I will give you the annotated version of this type of person's script. In the first few weeks of dating, the commitment-phobic person will come on very strong. He will pursue you ardently, and say all the right things, and take up all of your time. That is going to feel fantastic and you will feel like you have discovered the real thing. You will be out of your mind with joy. This will last for a bit, maybe three to six months——tops. The expiration phase will usually begin with something like, "I forgot to tell you I am going to Aspen without you. It's just the guys, and I knew you would understand." Inside you're going to feel angry and hurt, and he will tell you that there is nothing to worry about. He feels wonderful that you are being so understanding. You will be hurt and bury it, because he will be so charming and you will find a way to cope with this even though there was no original dialogue about it. He will come back a week or so later and there will be a slight change in the relationship. He might not be available this Saturday, which for the last few months was your time exclusively.

This is the beginning of him creating distance and you feeling very distressed and angry. You can try to present your upset, telling him more about your needs, though he won't pay much attention. You will start to feel like you are critical and nagging, but in effect, you feel like the safety in the relationship is dwindling. You will try to tell him about this, and he will tell you that you are crazy, that you are imagining things and he loves you more than life itself, and you believe it. Little by little, there will be moves where he does something without asking; a general lack of courtesy. The level of the commitment of the relationship goes down little by little. You are getting more hurt and more unsafe. If he is a true commitment-phobic person, you will ask him what's going on and he will probably say, "Nothing, everything's fine." Now you're going to be in a double-bind which is, if you believe that and go along with it, you are losing something inside yourself (self-respect); and if you don't believe him, then you have to break up with him. Either choice feels terrible.

There's also a middle way to deal with this, which is to take a little time-out in the relationship without saying it's over. It helps him to feel less threatened and maybe gives him some reason to not be so defensive and to think about things, especially if *you* suggest it. And it gives you time to see what this means to you. Go for a time-out. If your real fear is acting too decisively and cutting off any possibility of having a relationship, then this is a good choice. The only caveat I would add is that there should be a specific time limit. This way, you can get on with your life in a less wistful fashion if his behavior doesn't change.

Wow! How many times did I have to confront *that* script? What amazes me is how pervasive this dynamic is and that there is so little variation from story to story. The most important thing is recognizing it when it starts, and not letting it grow into a mini-series that lasts for more than one season. The most commitment-phobic men that I have dated were the most bold and forthright at the beginning of the relationship. They were the ones who asked me to help them pick out a new couch or kitchen cabinets and would sprinkle the all-important possessive pronoun "our" across very important sentences. The perfect example of this was when I was visiting my boyfriend Jake at his home in the country shortly after we met. We were sitting outside on his deck and having our second cup of morning coffee. He was talking about how he wanted to renovate the house, maybe build an addition, and landscape some of the back property. As he was winding down describing his vision, he looked at me and said, "Maybe we can sit down and figure it out together real soon." I gasped internally, and didn't know whether to be scared or thrilled. I heard that as "I am falling in love with you and we will be married soon and spend the rest of our lives together." After that exchange, little by little he began to recede, and the equivalent of the weekend in Aspen surfaced, and we eventually broke up. I was devastated because he had dangled this very appealing life in front of me before it was really appropriate to do so in relation to how long we had known each other and his capacity to commit at that time. To be fair, a few years later he married another woman within a year of meeting her, so perhaps my experience of him was not completely illustrative of who he was capable of being at another time in another set of circumstances.

While my courtship with my husband evolved in a completely healthy way, he was very prone to using the "our" word. I remember clearly that after he moved in to my apartment I would hear him say things like "Where is our milk?" or "Our car needs an oil change." He was commitment-centric and his saying things like that were indicative of where he really wanted the relationship to go. In contrast, I am someone who has a tendency to say "mine" or "my" versus "our" or "we." I find this to be very amusing in light of how much importance I had once put on the first person plural and how much I believed that it had a positive predictive quality to it.

conflict avoidance

I am basically a conflict-avoidant person and I have a great deal of trouble expressing conflict in a relationship. Is it better for one person in a relationship to be cool and the other to be hot? It seems like I date men who have no difficulties with conflict, yet I can't come to grips with it.

Conflict avoidance is a crippling thing to experience because it inevitably makes us feel frustrated and angry, mostly at ourselves. For some, conflict can be like quicksand, and the more you try to remove yourself from it, the more it devours and overwhelms you. It is unusual for any of us to have grown up in a family where it was entirely safe to express conflict. Oprah wasn't available prior to 1984 and few of us had the resources for therapy or even knew that avoiding conflict was a problem in the first place. If you grew up in a family where conflict led to violence or the threat of violence, then you will simply shut down when it comes to any kind of disagreement. You will swallow your feelings and tend to give in to something that doesn't feel good to you, because you won't want to rock the boat and risk disapproval. Then you will most likely become very upset, perhaps even filled with rage, at how the other person disregarded you and your needs.

Someone I used to work with struggles with this a great deal. His mother was married five times and he grew up with serial stepfathers who succumbed, one by one, to his mother's tarantula-like persona. As a result, he has a belief system that states "things need to end badly or they don't end at all." He cannot find middle ground between what he wants and what he is getting, so he shuts down and becomes resentful, acting out through deception and infidelity in the same way that his mother did with all of her husbands. When she had a problem with a spouse, she terminated the relationship or, conveniently, he died. College, marriage, and children did little to cultivate any conflict resolution skills.

Be careful if you are dating someone who never disagrees with you and rarely expresses his own preferences and opinions. Generally speaking, someone who cannot express conflict openly and honestly is in the running to become a future ex-husband.

I have struggled with this issue for a long time and, while it has gotten better, it has never fully gone away. It is something that continues to surface in all spheres of my life, both professional and personal. Presently, I have a business partner (as well as a close friend) who is not conflict avoidant when dealing with vendors or clients, but is very much so when dealing with things on a personal level. He once told me that he would rather have one big blowup than have to discuss and process things on a daily basis. On the one hand, this is convenient and comfortable, because it matches my own squeamishness around conflict. On the other hand, it is very unhealthy and creates an atmosphere where important feelings get deflected in the moment, but are unleashed in a very destructive manner later on. It is a delicate dance and one that has taught me a great deal about myself and the nature of conflict. I have very often been guilty of allowing him to go forward with something that I innately disagreed with, and then subsequently felt angry and resentful. Frustrated by his discomfort in dealing with his own turbulent feelings, he has often lashed out in ways that have hurt my feelings and created distance in our relationship. This is very difficult terrain to navigate when you sit next to each other all day and have no privacy in an office without walls. We have gone through apocalyptic moments and I consider it a bit of a miracle that we remain close and are genuinely fond of each other.

When it comes to conflict, the most valuable phrase and communication tool that I ever learned from a therapist was to say, "I have a dilemma." That really does make it possible to confront and defuse a potentially explosive and threatening situation, and allows the other person to hear you without being defensive. I have had many dilemmas and, stating them as such, have always made conflict less harsh than it might be otherwise.

control

How can I tell if someone has a controlling type of personality? Are all control issues bad?

Control has to do with domination, power struggles, and a shaky sense of self. Control is a way for somebody to manipulate a kind of powerfulness for themselves, because deep down they feel powerless, helpless—and perhaps unworthy. These are very negative feelings that come from a *very* negative sense of self. Control can be overt control, which is "do it my way, or else!" but I don't think most people operate that way. Control can also be subtler, which is manipulation. For instance, my friend's husband makes a scowling face every time she indicates she wants something that he doesn't. She's quite threatened by that face and eventually withdraws from what she wants and needs.

When we give up our own power in order to please our partner, that's him controlling us. If we live in terror of the consequences of not pleasing him——that's *out* of control. Of course at the end of all his controlling, the man has A) gotten what he wants, B) feels dominant, and C) feels momentarily good about himself after his conquest. Of course, it's never enough. There *will* be a next time.

Warning sign: the more you feel like you're giving up parts of yourself——your wants or your needs——with no feeling of having negotiated for yourself, the more you are going to feel his needs imposed upon you. You will feel that you have been controlled. However, if one of your core needs is to be subjugated or enslaved, you may not feel that you are being controlled. Perhaps that's what you saw in your family environment, or what you've become used to in order not to be abandoned by your family.

I learned all about the importance of control as a young child because I grew up in a family where anything could happen at any time. The first relationship that forced me to exert control was the one with my aunt (my mother's sister) who could be threatening when she was either sober or drunk. It was just more intense after she had been drinking. I remember grabbing the reins at five years old when we were taking a walk into town. I knew that I didn't want her to start asking me any uncomfortable questions, or——even more important——to hear any cutting remarks that she might make about me. So I flipped things, and asked her one question after the other. My first official interview! I was exhausted when we returned home, but felt like I had accomplished what I had set out to accomplish: complete and total insulation from her verbal abuse.

Because I had a mother who could control me with her crying and a father who could control me with his rage, I learned early that I had to develop my own means of control. Thus, I learned what other people liked or expected and I was able to present them with their preferences before they could ask for them. This skill endeared me to them, and gave me an edge. It wasn't until many years later that I realized the flip side to this emotional martial art—the loss of authenticity and spontaneity, which are crucial ingredients to having a full life. While it was a survival skill, it was manipulative and a difficult behavior to transform.

Control is the other side to trust, and the less we trust someone, the more control we want to exert. For the last several years I have witnessed the dissolution of a marriage that has exemplified this very issue. She is *very* artistic and ethereal and he is *very* pragmatic and earthy. For 20 years she relied on his ability to maneuver through life's daily challenges and he leaned on her for unconditional love and acceptance. As you might have guessed, this created a serious imbalance. Eventually, she felt more disempowered and he felt more oppressed. Figuratively speaking, he didn't trust her with taking the wheel, and he became more and more controlling over time. I remember one evening when they came over for dinner and my husband asked her if she would like to have a beer or a glass of wine. Before she could answer her husband said, "That's okay, she doesn't need anything to drink." There were many examples like this, and it just got worse over time.

Again, it all boils down to what we think we have to do in order to feel safe. With my aunt, I flipped from subject to subject because it protected me from her hurtful remarks. The now ex-husband of the aforementioned couple insisted on writing the checks because it kept them from being overdrawn at the bank. Now they are both with people who allow them to move toward the middle of the road. He is happy to have his new partner drive the car and his former wife has become more focused and self-reliant.

conversation

I have dated men who have talked only about themselves on the first few dates. Is this a preview of coming attractions?

Have you heard of narcissism? It means an excessive admiration or love of oneself. And it can be a narcissism alert if someone talks about himself so much that there isn't any room in him for curiosity about you. How much can he talk about his work? If he does interesting work, that's great, but even Nobel Prize scholars have to eat, go to the bathroom, watch TV, go out for dinner, and participate in conversation. If his achievements are always what is being discussed, then I would ask these questions: Do you feel that you've been related to? How much of your own needs and presence are being denied, smothered, or swallowed? By "swallowed" I mean feeling like you have to suppress chunks of yourself, and suppression usually blows up at some point. If you begin to rationalize, you're setting yourself up for marrying your future ex-husband, unless you're *willing* to be an uninteresting and suppressed personality. If you are a vicarious narcissist, getting your self-esteem from the achievements of others, all this will be familiar to you. You can lose yourself if you admire him continually and if he encourages that kind of admiration. One-way admiration gets tiring and worn out and that's when you're going to consider becoming an ex-partner.

Is conversation really that vital to a relationship? I have friends who seem happy and stable but say that they never really talk.

While it is true that some people are not very talkative, conversation is the main vehicle for relating. I have a friend who used to be frustrated when she would say things to her husband like "I had the most terrible dream last night" or "I can't believe how my father just spoke to me" and he wouldn't say "Really? Please tell me about it." He is a wonderful and loving person, but it wasn't natural for him to respond to her expressing her feelings in a way that made her feel listened to or cared for.

While some people are not natural-born talkers, I also believe that this can be a very male/female thing. A likely scenario is when a husband gets off of the phone with a friend, a wife will ask him a lot of questions like "Did they buy a new house?" or "What did they name their baby?" His usual response is "I don't know. They didn't say." While a woman is usually incredulous when this happens, she may come to accept it. While a husband can be good at tracking his wife's moods and feelings, he may not have that impulse when it comes to the outside world.

I've also worked with people who tell me that they and their partner do not speak to one another, except around things like going food shopping or walking the dog, or picking up the dry cleaning. If you are in a relationship where you truly can't or won't talk about the things that matter, then you have to ask yourself why this is comfortable for you. If you have grown up in a family where parents and children don't talk, then it is possible to replicate that experience by finding someone who recreates the original scenario, so you feel like you are back at home. The main thing here is if this is your choice and you are comfortable with it. If you are not comfortable, then address it or move on.

For me, conversation is an essential ingredient to any close relationship. If you were to ask my husband what he values most in our relationship, he would say "our conversations that begin with coffee at breakfast and end with wine at dinner." When we were first dating, I remember driving home from a movie with him and out of the blue he asked me, "What was your childhood like?" I was so surprised—even taken aback somewhat—because I had never been with anyone before who asked questions like that. I usually asked those kinds of questions.

I was certainly more comfortable being the "interrogator," which mirrored my MO with my aunt: take control and don't allow the other person to say or ask me anything that might make me uncomfortable.

A friend once made the astute observation that "Debra either interrogates you or ignores you." While I do enjoy conversations with those with whom I feel close, if I don't feel a connection, my petals fold and I withdraw. I just don't have the small-talk gene.

core needs

I have heard people talk about core needs. What are they? Are they critical to survival, or are they just learned preferences?

They are needs, primarily emotional and situational, that cannot be compromised without inducing strong feelings of deprivation. For example, if I am a quiet person and I absolutely need to be with someone who is outgoing and can draw me out, then that can't be easily compromised, or I will be giving up something that is really a profound part of me. It could also be compromising if I have a need to find somebody with integrity or reliability, and instead I find somebody who is always late and always has an excuse. If I find ways to rationalize a partner's behavior, then I am giving up or attempting to compromise my core needs for solidity, reliability, and integrity.

How do I identify my core needs?

There is no quick way. They are very personal and individual. An example: I need a lot of affection; I need a lot of touching. How often and how well does my partner have to respond to these needs? Well, suppose I find somebody I like who's not particularly affectionate and doesn't like a lot of touching? Then I have to see, without lying to myself, if that feels okay. Is that something on which I can compromise? You have to be honest and not delude yourself. Don't give up your core needs; take a lot of time discovering what they really are. Find out which core needs are negotiable and which are not. If you compromise the wrong core needs, you may end up regretting your decision. And in the long term, it will catch up with you.

I remember standing in the kitchen with a friend many years ago after observing an uncomfortable interaction between her and her husband. It was one of many, and I finally asked, "So what do you think it is that makes you want to stay together?" She thought for a moment and said, "Because he meets my core needs." When I asked her what they were she said, "To feel connected, to feel acknowledged and praised, and to feel loved." Several years later her husband moved on emotionally and asked for a divorce. Following his departure she said something like, "I never really felt connected to him in a real way. I could never be vulnerable. I always felt that I had to pretend to be someone else so he would love me. He made it very clear that I wasn't an equal and I never would be." There was trouble from the beginning when she wanted to keep her last name and he insisted that she take his. Her core need at the time was to feel loved and related to and that made it possible for her to rationalize what didn't feel good so she could stay in the relationship. Of course, there were also good things in their marriage that nurtured her and that supported and improved her functionality on a day-to-day basis. She didn't get a driver's license until many years after they married when he encouraged her to do so. Ultimately, her dilemma was in separating the wheat from the chaff, ie, deciding what was good and important from what wasn't healthy or meaningful anymore.

That seems to be the way that most of us eventually figure out our core needs.

criticism

I have dated men who were critical of other people as well as of our relationship. I may have seen it as being perceptive, when in fact it was downright mean-spirited. What does this kind of negative scrutiny signal? What is behind it?

A critical or sarcastic mode of communication is very threatening to the person who has to listen to it. Critical and sarcastic people use put-downs as a way of maintaining their power and dominance. Under this verbal bullying is an angry, insecure child. Critical men have issues involving power struggles. Chances are, their early power struggles with their parents, siblings, or others were never resolved and are now being transferred to you. You have to take a big leap of faith that this person is not going to put you down as he gets to know you better and love you more.

Another issue is you. How do you feel when your boyfriend criticizes you, or others? Upset or ashamed, hurt or angry? That is what is important to pay attention to. When you're attracted to a man, your alarm system could get suspended. Remember that your feelings are your survival pack, and if you are very needy, you can quickly lose your protective devices.

Like many young women, I thought when a man was being critical that he was really taking the time to be truthful and constructive. I remember in college when my first boyfriend rattled off a list of things that he didn't like about me: how I would say "What?" instead of "Excuse me?" when I didn't hear something he said, or how I didn't wear enough jewelry, and on and on. Predictably, he had low self-esteem and needed me to be perfect, to feel better about himself. He was also providing a replay of my father, who would either deify or demonize me depending on his moods.

Admittedly, I also sit on the other side of the table, and have spent most of my life being a relentlessly critical and judgmental person. I recently came upon a wonderful passage from the Midrash (the Jewish interpretation of biblical stories) that touched me deeply and enabled me to make some peace with this lifelong habit:

> "At first God thought to create the world through the quality of judgment, but realizing that the world could not endure at this level, God added on the quality of compassion." (Midrash Bereishit Raba 12:15)

Let me bring up my business partner again. Like me, he is by nature a very critical person. While I understand the origins of his harsh evaluations, it does not make it any easier to observe them or have my behavior be one of the things he is negatively evaluating. The only thing that has made it possible for me to maintain some grounding during our more stressful moments is the ability to go right to gratitude and compassion, which is not a very easy thing to do. I can become angry and critical of his behavior. But when I do, it plunges me into the depths of despair, as my self-righteousness does nothing for my immune system in the end, except enhance my susceptibility to more judgmental viruses. If I am not mindful it can become a vicious routine that depletes my emotional and creative energy.

cursing

I've dated men who curse a lot and it has often made me cringe. Is this something I should let go of or pay attention to?

Use of language is connected to appropriateness, which shows awareness of a context. A simple example: you wouldn't curse in church. If you find yourself undergoing a "cringe response" to your boyfriend's use of bad language, then something feels inappropriate to you. That response should never be ignored.

Inappropriateness of language, or other behaviors, signals insensitivity to surroundings. It can lead to you feeling humiliated in your environment and with other people. If the behavior is in character and done in appropriate places, then it's a matter of your own choice. Appropriateness is the price we pay to live in a cultured world. If someone doesn't respect this, then it must be taken seriously. Again, this can be easily rationalized by "he's just very honest" or "he's very direct with his feelings." It's a rationale for someone who has poor or insensitive social and personal boundaries.

Another hot button of my childhood. My father and his sisters cursed a lot——in both English and Yiddish. They all had very extroverted and volatile personalities, so I grew up thinking that it was normal for a grown-up to say things to me like "You selfish little son-of-a-bitch——I'm going to kill you if you don't clean your room!" Now it is simply unimaginable for me to think of anyone speaking to a child like that.

As much as I am often repulsed by cursing, I am also capable of a healthy dose of it myself. While I don't say things that are as deeply scarring and twisted as what my father would say, I am capable of infusing my verbal arsenal with profanity bullets now and then. My husband curses a lot, not at me, but at himself, or our cats. When he drops a piece of bread or a dish on the floor it is immediately followed by a "goddamn it" or "son-of-a-bitch!" I sometimes wonder if he thinks that cursing will make him taller. He is a thoughtful and kind man whose dark side is most easily revealed when stepping on, then cleaning up, cat vomit. He is a meticulous person who is easily derailed by unexpected stains. Thankfully this did not surface until many years of marriage. Had he cursed a lot in the beginning I don't think I would have felt very safe with him.

dependency

Sometimes I have felt way too dependent on a relationship to make me happy. But isn't that the point of a relationship—to feel connected to someone else so that you're no longer independent? I remember reading somewhere that it is important for the man to love the woman just a little more than the woman loves the man. So is it better for the man to be the dependent one?

We are in a country that has a Declaration of Independence, and perhaps that helped create a bias. Let's tell the truth: dependency has gotten a bad name. The fact is that we are all *inter*dependent. We rely on AT&T, we rely on the evening news, and we rely on the government's ability to safely maintain the infrastructure. We are dependent in our interpersonal needs as well.

We need other people!

We don't live in isolation. If we did, then we'd be like Ted Kaczynski, the Unabomber, or Henry David Thoreau. Even most people living at a 21st-Century version of Walden Pond still want electricity and running water and garbage collection. Today, we are globally interdependent. To try to pretend that we are not creates an unrealistic, unhealthy situation of psychological and physical isolation.

The real question that we want to deal with here is, "How autonomous should I be?" Dependency versus autonomy. In society, we have to make compromises in order to live together. The truth is, in our emotional lives, we are dancing a dance between needing other human beings and maintaining our autonomy. This isn't easy.

Our patriarchal society has been based on a system where women were dependent on men for their livelihood. There was some truth and practicality to this in earlier cultures, where women took care of the children. The Dependent Woman image reached its romanticized peak in the Victorian era, in which women were seen as childlike——not very wise or competent, and dependent on men for fulfillment of their needs. This concept was so entrenched at the time that Freud, the great father of psychoanalysis, created the idea of "penis envy."

Today we understand that if there is envy, it's not about having the penis, but having the power that goes along with it. And who can blame us? The idea of women as dependent contributes to the discrimination against women, and keeps them second-class citizens. Happily, this is changing. But what *hasn't* changed is that many women who don't marry may still feel dependent on men wanting them in order (they think) to fully claim their self-esteem. Also still with us is the Cinderella complex, coined in a 1981 book: trying to find a Prince Charming who will be able to protect us, take care of us, fulfill all our needs. (*The Cinderella Complex: Women's Hidden Fear of Independence* by Colette Dowling.)

Even today, many career women are characterized as not having a man in their lives. Some of these women have profound feelings of inadequacy and shame if they are not married by a certain age. They feel negatively judged by society. Even though we don't use the term "old maid" anymore, the stench of that phrase still lingers, and the fear of it leads to many bad marriages.

Dependency exists and functions on many levels: A) to have a husband, B) to confirm legitimacy, C) to have financial security, and D) to feel like an integral part of society. That's a heavy burden for women. A lot of research supports the fact that the two healthiest groups of people, both physically and mentally, are married men and unmarried women! This certainly indicates what contradictions women have had to live with. Often the scenario is, "I can be powerful in my office, but squeamish and powerless with my husband at home. I might even believe that I couldn't live without him." You don't often hear men say, "I can't live without her" except in the very early throes of romance or, much later, when their age and infirmities require a live-in caregiver.

Individuals each have their own threshold between healthy interdependence and healthy autonomy. It's not easy, but it's something that each woman has to find in herself, or within a marriage or relationship. If you don't find that balance, you can lose yourself and may find your boyfriend or husband judging you as being too clingy and not appropriately autonomous——or so independent that he feels superfluous.

Dependence is also related to fears of abandonment. I don't think it is necessarily better if the man is more dependent in the relationship, though it might confer a superficial level of security. If he's that dependent, then there will be something else that leaches out over time that won't feel comfortable. Moreover, if he is that dependent, then how can you trust his choices and his tendency to put your preferences before his own? After awhile that becomes tiring——especially for him, and he will likely resent you.

Though I have spent the better part of my adult life struggling with dependency issues and fear of abandonment, in and out of relationships, with the intention of finding the right one, I'm not sure that I really wanted to be married when I was a young girl. I remember playing with my Barbie® dolls and feeling embarrassed and humiliated at the thought of walking down the aisle. Maybe it was the wedding part and not the marriage part, but there was something going on inside that didn't propel me 100% into the prospect of being a wife. I was clearly ambiguous because I kept finding men who were not emotionally available, and the more unavailable they were, the more dependent on them I became. A recipe for disaster. I remember criticizing a friend who had married someone whom she didn't seem particularly passionate about. Meaning: she could have easily survived if he died or moved on, whereas when I thought of losing David, my priceless codependent boyfriend, I felt bereft and abandoned. What was it in me that made me see things this way? Why couldn't I see my friend as having healthier boundaries? I took the intensity of my codependency as proof of something noble and lofty, when in fact it was destructive and narcissistic.

Despite the difficulties of that relationship, I wasn't done yet. I still had many bridges to cross on my journey of self-actualization.

Flash-forward ten years: I met Jake, the engineer, poet, and artist. He lived in upstate New York and had an enviable life with a house filled with antiques, a big wonderful dog, a father who made chili on the weekends, and brothers with whom he regularly golfed. It was the perfect canvas upon which to project my longing and desire, thus sowing the seeds of the relationship's demise. It was hard to tell which was better—the physical intimacy or the serial letter writing——and I became very dependent on the feelings and projections that they both inspired. When the relationship ended I was in a tremendous amount of pain. The only way for me to swim from the depths of my sorrow was to accept it as a spiritual lesson that would help me to understand my impulses and tendency to get into these lopsided relationships.

Thankfully, I did not end up marrying someone who I was dependent on or who was dependent on me. In fact, I ended up marrying someone who was actually good for *me*. At times I do feel dependent, but not in quite the same way as before. It's more like I so thoroughly enjoy sharing my life with him, that it's impossible to imagine not being together. As someone who has had so much experience with loss, I often see the time code on the videotape. Princess Diana walking out of The Ritz Hotel with Dodi Fayed, not knowing that she only had minutes, not years, to live. I try not to indulge this part of me, that dreads separation and loss. But it is there, and I occasionally have to succumb to its impulses.

family relationships

Is it fair to evaluate someone's partnership potential based on my impressions of his family?

There's that great line from *The Godfather*: "That's my family, Kay, that's not me." Our parents are our first teachers, so when you meet someone's first teachers, you'll get a good idea about the school they went to and the education they received. It is totally valid to evaluate the kind of relationships that a man has with his family, especially his mom and dad. Often there are huge separation issues, better known as growing-up issues, ie, being able to move away from parents, emotionally and physically. It's important that your relationship with each other comes first. If that dominance isn't emphasized, there will often be a power struggle between the family of origin and your relationship. For instance, it is easy to feel grateful to be married and subdue our own needs.

If you are watching your potential future in-laws relate to each other in a way that doesn't feel good to you, it is an important issue to address. What feels negative? Do they relate that way with you? The unfinished business that parents have (or had) with each other can be transferred to your relationship.

When my dear friend Hannah was married to her future ex-husband he would consistently allow intrusions from his widowed mother. She would say subtly derisive remarks about Hannah right to her face, and her husband never stopped her. This continued for many years and was one of the main sources of conflict between them. This pointed to a larger problem that she was not fully aware of at the time. Eventually, these remarks escalated to open criticism about Hannah not agreeing to do certain things that the mother-in-law wanted, like visiting her with the children four times a week, even when she was working full time. After Hannah addressed the issue with her mother-in-law, to no avail, she finally reached her breaking point and insisted that her husband would have to put a stop to this. The husband said, "You can't ask me to choose between you and my mother." After they separated, he chided her for making the mistake of trying to force him to choose. She did ask him to take her side, and he was unable to do that. The unfinished business was that he hadn't fully separated from his mother. He dealt with his father's humiliation and disempowerment at the hands of his mother by trying to keep his wife controlled. By doing so, he was sustaining his father and keeping him powerful in front of his mother.

Is a man's relationship with his parents a crucial marker of what's to come in the relationship?

We can't ignore the fact that our families of origin create psychic imprints of how a family operates. All of us take that imprinting with us into adulthood. It would be valid to observe the family system, which has a predictive element to it. Often those dynamics get reconstructed in intimate relationships, and therapy can help erase these tapes.

What about someone who is estranged from his family or has few family connections?

You can't overly generalize, but you have to understand what caused the break. Were his parents alcoholics, or excessively selfish and mean-spirited, and thus unbearable to him? The context, however, might also point to somebody who sees the world in black and white and can't really find a middle ground on which to relate to his family.

This should alert you to the possibility that he easily polarizes in those two directions. As the saying goes, "If he's doing it to them, he'll do it to you."

What should one notice in how he relates to his mother? Attitude, affection, tone of voice?

If your boyfriend relates to his mother with respect, and feels that they are emotionally adult with each other, that's wonderful. If the mother exerts too much power and your boyfriend can be pushed around by her, or if her needs are more important than your needs, that is a red flag. Those things indicate that he is not appropriately separated from his mom. He hasn't grown up. Be careful if he still sees his mother with awe. This means he's had to suppress a lot of differences and conflict in order to grow up. There is some truth to the saying, "The way he treats her is how he'll treat you." So if you like what you see, great. If not, you have to ask yourself:

> Is his mother too important to him?
> Is he too much in awe of her?
> Is he overly sensitive to her wants and needs?
> Does he hate or disrespect her?

Whether he idealizes his mother or hates his mother, each side has its risks. The major risk is that he has no realistic image of his parent—she's either all good or all bad. He polarizes between love and hate. Eventually, you'll probably be caught up in that splitting process as well.

What about the father?

We are still looking at issues of idealization or vilification of a parent. What you want to look for here is how the father treats the mother. That's the template that's going to be important, because the interaction between the mother and father is the major internalized model for your boyfriend's relationships: often the dynamic between the parents will be reproduced by the son. If he's aware that the parents did not treat each other well, that is good, and leads to functional choices later on. Awareness in a potential partner is good, because it's the beginning of a dialogue about our differences. If someone is not aware that there are differences, there is no dialogue. Awareness is the ground for dialogue and working through differences.

Thankfully, my husband neither vilifies nor deifies either parent. While he is aware that they have not had the happiest of marriages, he is very empathic about what may be the reasons for their mutual and respective discontent. He acknowledges that they were very good to him, and he simply isn't interested in the details of their relationship——which is completely contrary to how I would feel in the same situation. The interrogator in me would want to deconstruct the family scripts. Clearly, he is a much more evolved person than I am!

His example is in stark contrast to my former boyfriend Arthur's feelings about his parents. When we first started seeing each other I had mentioned that my father was Jewish but my mother was not. He seemed delighted by the revelation, because it sort of made me a "Kosher shiksa." His parents were divorced and his mother had remarried. I had asked him to not get into the metrics of my Jewish DNA before I had a chance to meet her. Of course that didn't happen and he completely disregarded my request. He spoke to his mother several times a week, and in their native Hungarian. This meant that they had a "special" bond——they could communicate in a language that I could not understand. Predictably, she was disappointed before she even met me, which caused a schism in my boyfriend's psyche. His affection for me had made him a traitor to his mother, who by the way was not a matronly frump, but an exquisite, depressed woman who bore a resemblance to Ingrid Bergman. Could a girl ask for a better set-up for failure?

fit

What does "fit" actually mean?

Fit is profoundly important. It cuts to the whole continuum of life. For instance, is there a psychogical, narcissistic, or physical fit?

> A psychological fit: meaning, you like the way he is in the world and the way he relates to you. It makes you feel comfortable.
>
> A narcissistic *mis*-fit is, you have a PhD and are about to marry somebody who hasn't gone to college. It might not fit the way you want people to see you and the partner you've chosen.
>
> A physical fit? You're 5'1" and he's 6'4" . Well, that might be awkward, but it might not!

A person should fit or match the imprints you have within you. It's important to not ignore the issue of fit. The more fit there is, the more chance for a successful relationship. So if something tugs at you, that doesn't really fit for you, it's important not to ignore the validity of that feeling. My friend Hannah's future ex-husband was an Israeli, and they fit initially because she was Jewish as well. But that did not help with how scary and how difficult it was when they married and she was living in a new country. The commonality in religion didn't fully overtake the difficulties of living in a foreign land, another culture, and in a different language. But she deluded herself into thinking they were a possible fit.

There are many people we meet who are attractive and have wonderful qualities. However, that does not mean that they are a fit. I recently said to a friend who was grieving over a failed relationship, "If you need to have a partner who can hike in Tibet with you, then don't fall in love with someone who is terrified of heights." That may sound overly simplistic but this happens all of the time and you scratch your head dumbfounded, as if this is all new information. You have to be clear about what you need and what you want and if the person you are dating measures up.

While I firmly believe that most relationships can never be fully understood in earthly terms, some are more incredulous than others. Several years ago I had an interesting experience trying to understand this concept of "fit" regarding a couple that my husband had known for quite some time.

When I came into the picture they had been married for over ten years and I developed a real affection for them. On the surface they seemed completely divergent. Tim was a very conservative Rush Limbaugh fan who never read books, and Ivy was a socially liberal, fiscally conservative teacher who read about one book per week. In all of the time that they had been married, they never had been on a real vacation because Tim refused to take off the time from work. He was a laborer with a very well-paying union job and had a very unusual relationship to authority figures. He had somehow decided that he would never give his boss "the satisfaction" of requesting any vacation time. Of course this is utterly ridiculous and doesn't even make sense, but this was the prevailing mindset. Ivy put up with this and many other things that had the effect of drastically contracting the vitality of their relationship and most certainly their social life.

I would say that the most symbolic image of their union was the inside of their refrigerator. Compared to ours, which is overflowing with produce, cheeses, and leftovers, theirs was almost barren. I remember iced tea, milk, a bottle of salad dressing, mustard, ketchup, and little else. A mutual friend once went over for dinner and needed to get something from the fridge and later commented on this to me. He was simply astounded at how empty it was. It is important to note here that they lived a half mile from a major supermarket and Ivy would only shop on Monday (her day off). It didn't matter if they ran out of milk or coffee on Friday or Saturday, she wouldn't budge, and would wait until Monday to replenish what they needed. Flash-forward several years later when they moved to a very rural area that was about 30 minutes away from any kind of supermarket or food store. One day we were in the car with the Tim and I asked if they did a larger food shopping now since they were farther from any shopping areas. He said, "No, not really. Ivy only has two canvas bags, so she just buys whatever fits into them."

This is a great example of how what probably seems unacceptable to others was never a real problem for these two people. Their core need for security and predictability surpassed any need for intimacy, social connections, or travelling the world together. In the end, neither of them wanted or needed more than what could fit comfortably inside the two canvas shopping bags.

I must say that this notion of "fit" is something I have come to appreciate and not take for granted. My husband and I have (at least in my opinion) an unusual degree of fit. Aside from having the same appreciation for books, art, music, and travel, we share an odd set of childhood preferences. We both stayed up late at night watching movies our parents would have thoroughly disapproved of had they known. One of them was the film *Let No Man Write My Epitaph* with Shelley Winters and Burl Ives. It was a bleak study of downtrodden junkies whose lives didn't get better as the film wore on. It left me feeling frightened but riveted. I couldn't turn off the TV. My husband had the same response when he watched it as a child. On a happier note, we both loved talk shows and were stalwart fans of Johnny Carson, Merv Griffin, and Dick Cavett.

Perhaps the best illustration of fit is my husband's description of our relationship: "It is edge, without edge."

helplessness

I know many women who have been attracted to men who seem helpless, at least initially, in innocuous ways. The men need someone to come over and sort their bills, straighten their shelves, clean out the fridge, etc. Why do some women find this type of guy attractive, since it would seem very suffocating and tiresome to me—at least now?

Women who are attracted to helpless men have control issues. While the helpless piece of it may be annoying and exhausting, the bottom-line need that is getting met is control—over everything. Healthy adult relationships are about mutuality, where you can depend on each other for cover and companionship. In the helpless-man situation, the woman eventually becomes the parent and probably morphs into an angry and indifferent parent after awhile. Presumably we choose people to partner with in order to get our needs met. If all we are doing is meeting the needs of the helpless man, then who is meeting our needs? In some cases this may be irrelevant because the woman is more concerned with being in charge and calling the shots. This is the beginning of a corrosive history that will set a terrible example of relating if children are involved. Children will perceive the imbalanced dynamic between the parents, and will most likely act out on behalf of one or both of them. A friend of mine was once married to a helpless type of man. Her five-year-old son would bite his father all of the time, even though the father acted lovingly toward the child. The boy was acting out his mother's resentment, which she never owned up to directly. The couple eventually divorced and the now grown son has endured a series of unhappy relationships. He finds women who are much like his mother and he has a repulsion/attraction response to them. While the mothering is familiar, it is also disempowering and he eventually becomes resentful and breaks up with them.

Is he helpless in those relationships?

He alternates between being domineering and passive. The domineering phase is connected to his desire to avoid his father's fate, and the passive phase is about the comfort and predictability of being with a controlling woman. Ultimately, it is a barrier to any authentic intimacy because he's never developed any healthy independence. My friend Franco refers to controlling mothers (like his Roman mother and aunts) as "Supermamas"——women who hold their children hostage emotionally. If the child moves toward any sort of autonomy the mother pulls back and expresses disappointment or——worse——withdraws all affection and approval, which will make the son relinquish any thoughts of moving on without her.

Looking back, I can see that two former boyfriends, David and Arthur, had Supermamas and they did alternate between being domineering and passive, though not explicitly helpless. I've already addressed Arthur's mother, who wielded control by expressing her disappointment. David had a mother who washed his meatballs for him. Seriously. When he was young he didn't like tomato sauce so she would rinse the meatballs she made for him under the faucet so that he would eat them. She was a verbally imposing presence who never stopped barking. She had a special brand of mothering that made her son feel special and guilty all at the same time. He once told me that when he and his older sister were fighting, she slapped his sister then sent them to their own rooms. A few minutes later she marched into to her son's room, feigning anger, and pretended to hit him by slapping herself on her leg while saying, "Don't ever speak like that to your sister again!" This was a vivid memory for him and it left him feeling very uncomfortable. That gesture created an inappropriate intimacy between them. She had explicitly demonstrated that her sympathies were with him and not his sister, and it made him feel guilty that he was her favorite.

Here are two perfect examples of how all of this played out in our relationship. When we would go out to dinner and it was time to order,

David would inevitably say, "Why don't you just order for both of us?" He would never choose for himself and it was maddening. Of course, when he didn't like what I had ordered, he became angry and blamed me for selecting the wrong thing. Worse was whenever we would get lost while driving and he would stop to ask for directions. He would roll down the window, listen intently to what the person was telling him and then turn to me and say, "Deb——you got all of that——right?"

You simply can't win, so the best thing to do is leave!

humor

I know that, for me, a sense of humor is critical, but I have had boyfriends with a great sense of humor, and it ended up meaning nothing in the end. Are there different "senses" of humor a person can have?

Humor is a positive variable in successful mating, but if the humor is at someone else's expense and is closer to mockery, then beware! If the humor is coming from an awareness of the absurdities of the human condition, and if the feelings between the two of you are those of friendship, fun, and liveliness, then humor is a great predictor of a successful future marriage. Mockery, or black humor, or, worst of all, if the humor is at your expense——then run for the door! Humor that makes healthy fun of what it's like to be human is a guarantee of a long marriage. Good humor defuses conflict and anger so a healthy repair can occur. Laugh a lot.

My husband has a very dry sense of humor and puts the "bon" in bon mots. He is someone who truly can "sense" the humor in even the most dire of situations. This has made it possible for us to weather many storms. For me, a sense of humor implies that it is possible to deal with the mind-bending challenges that life throws our way. An absence of humor can be related to feelings of anxiety or paranoia, neither of which serves to fertilize the soil of a new relationship. In short, it is a good sign when someone can make you laugh, or even better, calm a stormy moment by not taking things too seriously and being able to see beyond the immediate difficulty.

In my business, we have gone through many ups and downs, and cash flow is always an issue. Once I laughed when a senior staff member was catastrophizing about the situation. He threw up his hands and said, "If you can laugh about this then you are a stronger person than I am!" Humor helps us survive.

internet dating

So many people I know have met their partners online. What about trusting the information you read on someone's profile? Should you always be open to finding out for yourself if someone is as good as he appears online?

Be cautious.

Nothing seen on an Internet dating site should be believed. You must meet the person in order to even have any initial idea of what the truth might be. The Internet is like a resume: can you believe everything on a resume? The little white lies are magnified!

I have a great deal to say about Internet "dating." For some women it is comfortable to cultivate an online relationship that thrives on the immediacy of e-mails and instant messaging. But the absence of real contact for a protracted length of time often encourages an enormous amount of projection that can produce catastrophic results.

Here is an example of a woman who became involved in such a relationship. She had posted a personal ad on a Jewish singles Web site. Shortly thereafter, a divorced father of three contacted her. Despite the fact that he lived four states away, and she had told him repeatedly that she wasn't interested, he continued to e-mail and instant-message her. They finally began speaking on the phone, and that's when a cycle of events began that would involve her losing $30,000, her stellar credit rating, and a good amount of her sanity. He told her he was a former Navy SEAL who had lost most of his money to his ex-wife in many court custody battles. He also said that he was in the process of converting to Judaism; his former wife was an ex-member of the American Nazi party; and yes, he was a devoted dad who took his kids to their ice skating lessons. Their courtship began during the 2000 war in Kosovo, and he told my friend that in order to pay back child support and avoid going to jail, he would have to go over and fight in the Balkans, leaving his three children for an undetermined amount of time. He basically set things up in such a way that my friend offered to lend him $15,000 for the child support arrears so he could stay at home and tend to his children.

Guess what? After she loaned him the $15,000 he told her that if he didn't want to get "drafted" again, he would need what the U.S. government considers a critical job such as law enforcement, medical work, or transportation/trucking. Trucking? Yes, he told her that trucking was considered a critical job, and if he were to start up his own trucking company, it would prevent him from being recruited for future foreign wars. She ended up financing two trucks for him, met him only two times on his turf, and never even kissed him romantically.

As it turns out, he was a convicted felon, had been married eight times, fathered many children, and was a Grand Dragon of the Ku Klux Klan. While it is true that many people have found wonderful partners on Match.com, let this be a cautionary tale.

interrogation

I have dated men who sometimes have that tendency to interrogate instead of just asking questions and it can feel very threatening. What is the best way to respond to something like that in the first few months of dating? Is it something that should be overlooked if everything else seems wonderful?

While context is important, intrusiveness of any kind is worrisome, and of course much of this is related to boundaries. Some people like to ask more questions than others and are often not satisfied with the answers they are given. It depends on the nature of the questions and what they are related to. If a man is asking you for excessive amounts of detail about mundane activities, then I would ask him what doesn't feel satisfying about what and how you have communicated a particular event to him. What wasn't he hearing that made him think there was more to tell?

A friend of mine talks in her sleep and one night her boyfriend heard her laughing and woke her up to ask her what she was laughing at. She mumbled something like "I don't know" and tried to get back to sleep. He insisted on waking her up asking her a lot more questions about the laughing. It escalated and she finally told him to back off and that there was nothing she could tell him about why she laughed. This caused him to sulk for a while and then he finally came around. Is an exchange like that indicative of trouble ahead?

In the early stages of dating you are feeling each other out and building layers of trust as you move through each episode that brings you closer to knowing the other person. Interrogating other people stems primarily from trust issues. If a man you are dating is exhibiting excessive amounts of this in the early stages, there is a strong chance that he has some serious issues around trust. Even mild ambiguity can set him off and produce a profound amount of anxiety, and he will press on as a way to quell that anxiety. Of course, it's entirely possible that garnering more information has the opposite effect and winds him up even more when he can't uncover an answer that feels "right." We *ask* for directions and we *interrogate* suspects, so there is the suspicion and mistrust thing that comes up with this. Asking should never be confused with interrogating. If a man is doing more of the latter and less of the former, then it might be a good idea to move on to a less intense type of person.

I was once very close with someone who interrogated people quite frequently. Thankfully we were not romantically involved, but we were good friends. One evening we were at dinner and he was obsessing about something with his new car——along the lines of "Was the leather on the driver side as soft as the leather on the passenger side?" He kept going on and on and I finally said something like, "You remind me so much of my old boyfriend David. He would buy a shirt at the store, and then spend the next three hours examining it for imperfections." I said it very casually and he heard it very critically and proceeded to interrogate me for the next two hours. He questioned, "Why would you compare me to David and assume that my intention was the same as his intention?" and on and on and on. He became very hostile, and his energy became very threatening. Because of the skills I acquired growing up in my family, I was able to stay calm and restore his sense of equilibrium and neutralize his feeling of being condescended to by my remark. It was exhausting! Shortly after that he became involved in a very intense, very tumultuous relationship where similar patterns emerged. He would spend hours, days, and weeks interrogating his new girlfriend over remarks or observations that she shared. Ambiguity of any kind was intolerable for him. It really produced a severe amount of anxiety that no amount of his questioning could ever appease. He had to drain every drop of juice out of his partner's batteries before he could safely disengage.

jealousy

I have never dated someone who was jealous of me, but I have felt very jealous at times, and that has made me feel insecure and needy. Is jealousy ever legitimate? Is it ever not a destructive impulse?

Jealousy is a blood relative of narcissism, the inadequate sense of self related to our feelings of insecurity and anticipated loss. There is an implied threat when we are jealous of someone else, ie, whatever *they* have is taking, or will take, something away from *me*. What gives jealousy so much power is the underlying feeling that we don't believe that we can get the object of our desire for ourself. If we can buy an expensive pair of shoes, there is no reason to feel jealous if we notice someone wearing a gorgeous pair of designer shoes. However, if we feel like there is no way we will ever be able to walk into a store and walk out with what we want, then it is likely that we will feel jealous. What flips the jealousy switch is how much (or how little) we believe in our power to acquire or achieve what we want. The more inadequate we feel, the more jealous we are likely to become.

Of course there can be real triggers for jealousy, like if the man you have been dating for two weeks keeps taking calls from other women or talks a lot about past relationships. With a healthy sense of self, it will start out as jealousy, but will quickly transition into disgust when your self-esteem steps in to remind you that this is not appropriate. Unbridled jealousy, the kind that leads to physical violence, is sociopathic, and should never be tolerated. Not for one second. Today we read about celebrities who call the cops during a violent row, often triggered by jealousy. Then we see them three days later at the Oscars looking like nothing ever happened. It is unfortunate that this kind of behavior is modeled, especially for young women. Is jealousy ever not a destructive impulse? I think not, because it fundamentally implies a lack of trust in the other person, and most definitely in you.

If you are dating someone who is very jealous and suspicious, who doesn't trust you, and wants to read your text messages——it's a sure bet that he is a future ex-husband.

I have experienced both being jealous and the companion piece—not believing that I had the power to attain what I was coveting. A few years ago I attended a colleague's birthday party. A few minutes after I got there I saw a woman arrive in a white BMW sedan, and it turned out to be a person who I used to work with many years before. At that time, she was a recent college graduate, hired for an entry level position. I felt completely deflated seeing her, and immediately collapsed into what a failure I was because I wasn't driving an expensive car. In the moment, it didn't matter that I owned my own company and did a million other things that most people never do, and things that *she* certainly had never done. What only mattered was that I believed that her car was indicative of a level of professional success that somehow eluded me. Of course, the entire thing was ridiculous and the absurdity was revealed several months later when she sent me an e-mail telling me that she had been laid off from her job and was looking for a new one. Preferably with my company!

There have been times in past romantic relationships when I have felt acute jealousy, usually around the feeling of not being included. One time I made plans to visit Jake for Memorial Day weekend, and I had mentioned beforehand that I would arrive on Friday and most likely leave on Sunday. So Sunday rolled around, I made pancakes for breakfast for the two of us, and then his brother and sister-in-law came over to visit. They all started talking about playing golf later that afternoon. I began to sulk inside when it was clear that I wasn't included and that my stay would not be extended upon request. I immediately went into my hurt mode and began to withdraw. I felt jealous and angry that I wasn't asked to join them. These feelings were intensified when he suggested that I stop at an outdoor sculpture park on my way home. I was infuriated and doubly hurt that he didn't want to share that experience with me. Looking back, I can be a bit more generous. I guess that it is possible that he thought that I had a life apart from spending time with him, and perhaps I wanted to get back to it before the work week resumed.

It really is painful to think about these past episodes but it is a relief that I experience them less and less as time goes on——thankfully!

lateness

My best friend is dating someone who is frequently late for their dates and it sometimes drives her over the edge. Is she overreacting? People are very busy and life can be chaotic these days, so is lateness ever an excusable thing?

No, she is not overreacting. Consistent lateness is a passive-aggressive trait. My definition of passive-aggressive behavior is this: somebody kicks you, and then gets angry with you because *their* foot hurts! Lateness is a kick. It's not only passive-aggressive, but also belongs with control issues. I think when it consistently happens, you're either dealing with a flake, an unconsciously passive-aggressive person, or an intentionally aggressive one. When he is late, of course he tries to minimize your upset, and this can be a sign of deeper issues. If lateness is happening, consistently, regardless of his excuses, run.

People who are chronically late are chronically self-absorbed. I know someone who is never on time to meet with her clients, forgets the keys to her office, and takes calls on her cell phone during meetings. Another friend is the complete opposite. In fact, she is so anxious about being on time, that she is usually very early. She values her time and is respectful of others. However, this has often produced an anxious feeling in me if I thought I would be late in meeting her someplace. I tend to be more like her, and my breathing gets more rapid when stuck in traffic. I am not someone who leaves for the airport 30 minutes before my flight.

In the first few weeks or months of dating, it is important to be on time because that is a preview of coming attractions and how reliable a person is and how well they manage their time. If they can't be on time and they renege on such a simple agreement, what will they be like when it comes to more important things? Promptness is about reliability and consideration. Period.

lying

When I was younger I used to lie. Are there degrees of lying? Like, is a white lie different from a black lie? Does context and a fear of hurting the other person's feelings matter?

Lies can be divided into two types: white lies, which essentially run civilization, and those that may be called "characterological" lies, which means it's everybody to their own lies, or the lies they can tolerate. You really have to judge which is which. Characterological lying is telling lies even when there is the choice to tell the truth without being punished——the first impulse is to lie, to avoid the truth and its attendant discomfort. It's about avoidance of both feelings and the consequences of behavior.

I recently worked with someone who had a boyfriend who claimed that he worked with Noam Chomsky at M.I.T. Naturally she was very impressed, but it was a lie. I see that kind as a characterological lie. It came from his own awful feelings about himself, but she wasn't his therapist, and he wasn't her patient. The nature of the lie is important, but as one of my great teachers said, "Once is an accident, twice is a trend, and three times is a process." You might be able to forgive the first, excuse the second, but then three strikes and he's out.

Because I grew up in a very temperamental family, it wasn't always safe to tell the truth. So I learned at a very early age that I could manipulate reality by altering it. If I broke a toy and my father found out, it was likely that I would be smacked, so the easiest, most practical thing to do was lie and say, "No, I didn't do it." So lying not only got me out of an immediate pinch, but it also revealed a certain power that I had over my elders that was a bit gratifying. The problem is that it can become an unhealthy habit, and you have to be mindful and discriminate between the white lies and more serious ones. If I think back about the times I have committed the latter, it was due to a specific feeling of fear and discomfort, and yes, an avoidance of feeling. Carrie Fisher has said that we are only as sick as our lies, and since I no longer want to be in that place, I try to tell the truth as much as possible. It is still difficult for me to be completely honest with a friend if I don't like something that they have cooked, written, or drawn, because I don't want to hurt their feelings. I've given myself permission to make that discrimination.

manners

I've often found that someone's manners are a very important clue to how they relate to the world around them. Is there any truth to that?

Picture dating somebody who chews with his mouth open. It is not a pleasant experience to see the half-chewed hamburger in his mouth, or to hear him slurping coffee, or worse, not to hear him say "thank you" or "hello" or "please." You can deal with manners if your partner is willing to hear what you have to say about his and is interested in changing. If what you have to say is met with defensiveness, or anger, then walk, or accept the fact that you'll have to live with it. If the issue is inept manners, I think that can be dealt with if your partner is ready to learn.

Manners were very important in my family when I was growing up. My mother had an etiquette book that she would pull out often, to reinforce how one should cut meat, chew, and essentially behave like a civilized person in public. This made me very curious and observant when it came to the table manners of my friends, and more often than not, their mothers hadn't taught them to cut the meat properly. They would stab the meat with their fork, as if they were going to carve a turkey instead of slicing a piece of steak. My first boyfriend David did know how to cut a steak and I was impressed by that. A friend I grew up with does the stab method, as do most people I know——except my husband. The worst thing for me is public flossing. I would never be able to feel good about someone who flosses their teeth at their desk, on the train, or in a restaurant.

While manners are definitely an important cue they aren't always an accurate representation of a person's partnership potential. I remember stopping at a convenience store one evening with Nicky, who I had been dating for about a month. I don't recall what we stopped for but I waited up front for him while he walked around. When he got back he had a can of Diet Coke in his hand. He remembered that I liked it and picked it up without me even suggesting that he do so. I was very touched by that and immediately began to fantasize about marrying him. As time wore on these gestures appeared less and less and eventually it all fizzled.

My husband has wonderful manners that remind me of how incredibly unconscious and self-absorbed *I* am capable of being.

married men

A very close friend of mine has been dating a married man for eight years who has been living apart from his wife for the past decade or more. He and his wife have three adult children who the wife uses to manipulate him emotionally whenever he speaks of a formal separation or divorce. My friend is also aware that he had many affairs during his marriage. What should she do?

First I would ask, what drew her to this person? Especially when she knew he had a long marriage, with a subsequent history of unfinished relationships that never came to real fruition. It sounds like she did ask him about obtaining a formal separation or divorce from his wife, and when he was pushed against the wall, he found a reason not to do it. Commitment is scary for him.

It is of the utmost importance that your friend look at her own fears of closeness and her own feelings of desperation. She went into a relationship that already had a lot of questions swirling around it. And what were the promises that he made? How did she handle it once she knew what his background was?

Should he be given an ultimatum?

Let's agree that if things have gone on this long, there is certainly an issue. I'm not a believer in ultimatums. I think the first step is to have a clear dialogue on the nature of what his difficulties are about formally leaving his marriage. She should try to be empathic, and listen carefully to what he says. He must own his fears of feeling terrified with his wife's threat that "the children will have nothing to do with you if you divorce me." This is emotional blackmail and raises questions about why he's given in so quickly to this blackmail, especially when his children are grown and married. He's really seized the moment by exploiting the wife's blackmail. There's something that feels a little sneaky about that.

He is commitment phobic. The issue is not in being married, but in his need to create distance in the relationship. In this case, there is one married man who has two relationships and maintains the distance on both sides, for the wife and the lover. Even if he wildly loves your friend, there is still the issue of the underlying distance. He's not fully available.

These men usually have had a parent (probably the mother) who was either absent or devouring, and their current defense is against being devoured and/or abandoned. The defense is what I call an "isolating defense." So what you have is a cover for the guy, who is married, as he avoids being either devoured or abandoned by maintaining distance and not having one full partner. He creates a little vacuum around himself, so no one can really get too close.

There are two ways to handle this: to confront the man with his isolation defenses and to have a talk with him about his hesitancy toward the next step. He will either isolate himself or cultivate defenses against being devoured. Again, everything will be fine until you come out with a serious want or need, which he will experience as feeling devoured. Ask him what else he needs to make this decision. What has to happen to help him make this decision?

If you have never been married and you are dating or living with a married man, you need to look at your own isolation defenses. Why do you find men who are not fully available? Why are you involved in a relationship that doesn't, and can't, go "all the way?" You can't have a real relationship when there's an elephant in the room. It's not easy. The elephant has to be confronted, and most urgently if it's a situation you have found yourself in more than once.

If you have been married and have had children and you are dating a married man, well, I think that there is a big difference. This is not the place to be if you want your own marriage and a commitment. If the presence of another man's wife is not intimidating, and you are able to truly get past it, then go ahead. If the marriage is a thorn, then you must end this relationship or live with a lot of hurt and disappointment. Do you think you're worth so little that you should be content to be just the icing on some married man's cake?

money

In my relationships, I have found that the other person's attitude about money was a crucial indicator of their emotional generosity. Is that too broad a generalization to make?

Money is really the code word for love and power. Our culture puts tremendous weight on the amount of money you have. It's directly connected to your value as a person. In our culture, we tend to worship people who've made a lot money, without any serious understanding of their character. Money often is the substitution for childhood deficits in love. So stinginess with money correlates with stinginess with emotions and caring.

People who are stingy can't give easily, and what seems tolerable to you in the beginning——again a rationalization——later becomes the source of conflict. You may feel like you're living in an emotional desert where his withholding the water is the name of the game. Eventually, you become very thirsty, and in these circumstances, your feelings dry up. At that point, all attempts by you to fix this situation usually won't work. It's too late—deposits made in his love bank by his parents were insufficient. No matter what you give it will not be enough to fill his bank, and he can't give what he never got. Another part of stinginess can be trauma which is different from being overly careful with money. Stinginess smells like withholding. Someone who is "careful" with money is possibly dealing with anxiety about money due to early trauma.

I need to bring up my friend Hannah again, because her story is very characteristic of this issue. There were many signals around money in her former marriage that she chose not to pay attention to. For example, her husband's problems with being generous first surfaced over the wedding ring. She sensed that it would be a problem if she wanted something expensive, so she picked out a $40 ring and then asked herself, "Why can't he give me what I want without me feeling guilty or angry?"

Of course she saw his difficulties in being generous from the very beginning, but never allowed herself to openly address it. She saw it as something wrong with *her*. Maybe she was spoiled, maybe she was being too much of a Jewish princess. She *rationalized* it over and over again. She ignored how characterlogical it was.

What about guys who are the opposite—very showy and excessive?

Lavishing is the other side of the coin, with two aspects: buying love and showing off. In the later stages of a blossoming relationship, when trust and understanding have grown, then lavishness can be a natural part of showing love and caring. However, in the beginning stages, when it is exaggerated, when you have no words for the beautiful piece of jewelry on the third date, or the great restaurants you've been to, your inner alarm will get triggered. You sense that the lavishness has nothing to do with you and everything to do with what he needs to do so he can feel good about himself.

If the interviewer James Lipton asked me, "What is your least favorite word?" I would say "stingy." I can't stand the sound or the smell of it. Money was a strange thing in my family of gamblers and wise guys. My father would think nothing of handing me a $5 or $10 bill in front of my friends, suggesting that I treat everyone to ice cream. One of my uncles would always reach into his pocket after I kissed him hello and put $20 in my hand. A friend's father once ripped a $10 bill in half in front of a group of eight-year-old kids to show how little money meant to him. The irony here is that we never really had a lot of money, so showing off was everyone's way of feeling like we did. I have inherited this worldview to some degree. I'm rarely comfortable splitting the check with a friend——it's simply easier to pay for the whole thing, and I suppose it makes me feel generous and solvent the same way it made my father feel to have 30 pairs of shoes in his closet.

As far as relationships go, I have experienced both the sting of stinginess and the discomfort of flagrance. I was dating someone who was doing fairly well at the time and I was in between jobs, temping while looking for full-time employment. He was telling me about this wonderful restaurant in Manhattan that he wanted to take me to, with the caveat that we would have to go Dutch because it was very expensive. That hurt my feelings and made me feel less loved.

Arthur infused the first six months of our dating with weekends at opulent bed & breakfasts, lavish dinners, and expensive wines. I remember that I had a cold for about three months, and traveled to meet him in various places with this pricey bottle of champagne in my luggage. We never opened it on any of these occasions because I never felt well enough to drink. Looking back, I believe that my immune system was trying to communicate to me a very important truth——that he was focusing on these upscale accoutrements more than he was addressing his escalating fears about commitment. He was very generous with money, but also very reckless. I remember him throwing out produce from the refrigerator with glee, which I found offensive and wasteful. He shrugged his shoulders and said, "Why feel bad when I can just buy more?"

narcissism

There's so much written about narcissism and most of it is difficult to understand. What is it really—in plain English?

A narcissist is someone who is self-involved, and underneath the self-involvement is a very scared person with a very inadequate sense of self. They often have little empathy, which means they can't easily relate to the needs of another. They tend to be attractive and attracted to people who will make them feel good about how they would like to see themselves. Narcissists need to control other people as a way of fighting off their own scary and inadequate feelings. So you can have a fine relationship with a narcissist if you don't have any important differences with him and if you physically and emotionally represent what he can admire. Narcissists need to be admired and/or perfect. Therefore, being their love object, you have to be admirable and perfect. So the trouble comes down the road when the differences begin to emerge, ie, you gain five pounds or you're paying too much attention to the baby. They look at you as an object to help them feel good about themselves. It's not about you.

If you feel controlled by somebody, and this person doesn't show any real interest in you or your feelings, and needs to dominate, he is probably a narcissist and a good candidate for your future ex-husband.

How do you distinguish between healthy and unhealthy narcissism?

Healthy narcissism is a strong positive sense of self, most of the time, and a stable sense of self, even in difficult times—being able to go with the ups and downs in life without crashing, without a sense of your inner self crashing.

I grew up in a narcissist's garden that programmed me to be wildly attracted to anyone I met whose scent resembled my former landscape. One of my earliest memories of being snagged by the narcissist's claw was when I was five years old. My parents had some friends and their children over and there was music playing and we all began to dance. All of a sudden my father lunged at me and said, "Stop doing that! Don't ever do that again!" Of course I was embarrassed, and it would take me many years to dance in public again. This is one of many examples of where my needs were displaced or overlooked in deference to my father's narcissism.

Many years later during my rather intense adolescence, I began to write poetry——the typical fare that depressed teenagers write: "I woke up this morning stapled to my bed/Hugging my pillow wishing I were dead… ." So one day I decided to share my writing with my father. He read the poem, slapped his hand against the table and exclaimed, "Son-of-a-bitch, and here I thought you were the happiest kid in the world!" What he was upset at was not my depression, but that I disrupted his narcissistic need to see me in a certain way that made him feel better about his parenting.

passive-aggressive behavior

I feel as if I am a magnet for passive-aggressive behavior and I am puzzled why it is such a persistent theme in my life. How can I better understand passive-aggressive behavior?

Passive-aggressive people are still having unresolved power struggles with their parents. They are angry about being angry and about having to struggle. This is the kick phenomenon again——they kick you and then get angry with you because their foot hurts. This type of behavior shows up as a feeling that you are in a constant power struggle with them. For instance, you want to go to the movies, he wants to stay home. Instead of having a discussion about this, you find yourself feeling angry inside and that it's wrong to want what you want. Passive-aggressive people tend to withhold, and they get *pleasure* in withholding and torturing.

Passive-aggressive men are very angry and demanding. They will use many creative provocations to get you angry, and then become angry at your anger. There will also be many confrontations, usually telling you how disappointing you are, especially if you don't follow their wishes. If you jump to their provocations, you will let yourself become involved in a power struggle with them——and that is a formula for creating your own anger and feeling totally misunderstood and frustrated.

A very dear friend of mine is in a classic passive-aggressive relationship. Whenever his girlfriend is angry or upset, she will get up and leave the room, hang up the phone, or withhold something (like the car keys, sex, approval, etc.) rather than behaving like an adult.

I believe this type of behavior is cultivated by growing up in a family where it isn't safe to get angry, because one or both parents withdraws or signals that it isn't okay to feel what you feel, especially if it's negative. My friend's partner is someone who reminds people about wearing their seat belt after they've gone through the windshield. Whether it is conscious or not, it is clearly destructive. It's sort of like "if I don't have the power to create, then I certainly have the power to destroy and disrupt. Watch out." If you notice this type of behavior in the first trimester of dating——move on to healthier ground.

past relationships

What if a man tells you a lot about his previous relationships? It's hard for me to distinguish between someone sharing information about his life versus inappropriate disclosures. How do you identify the difference?

Look, we all have pasts, but do we dump our past in the present when we first meet somebody? You have to ask yourself why previous relationships come to light in the first few meetings. That shows where his concentration lies. The issue is, how he talks about them. I once went out with someone and he mentioned that he had a long relationship with a model. He mentioned it quite a few times. I wasn't a model and it made me feel somehow inadequate, because I believed that in some way he was boasting about having been with a gorgeous woman, and comparing me to her. I didn't ask him to tell me about this, but he did. I couldn't understand his motive for telling me on our first date, other than to show off. He was giving me information I really didn't need at that moment. But if a man talks about previous relationships with a retrospective stance and that they were "learning" relationships, then you are not in danger of marrying your future ex-husband.

How should a woman evaluate her boyfriend's relationship history?

It's important to take his relationship history. You want to find out what defeated previous relationships, and how long they lasted. The biggest issue really is what your boyfriend is saying about the end of the relationships. Be careful when the old girlfriend or wife gets trashed. That will be you around the bend. If your history and his history have been primarily in pain-based relationships, then you're going to be very attracted to each other. History is a marker, pointing to processes that have occurred. If a person has an awareness of his process and an interest in changing it, that is a good sign. If the person hasn't an iota of understanding, and only blames the failures on his ex-girlfriends—run as fast as you can. Blaming is one of the great causes of divorce. If you're being blamed and criticized in a relationship, then look out.

I do have friends who have experienced someone gushing about a past relationship and it was very unsettling for them. It would seem that someone would do this to keep you off-balance and make you feel inadequate from the beginning. There's a big difference between positively acknowledging a past partner and waxing on about her great body or her brains. It's healthy when people don't trash their former mates and it's unhealthy when they extol them compulsively. When a man puts down his prior relationships it is one of those all-important signals that he is not very secure and is "conditioning the atmosphere" to inflate his sense of himself.

pornography

Should I feel threatened if someone I am dating enjoys pornography?

Pornography doesn't mean anything by itself, but excessive amounts of it can point to possible compulsions and obsessions, and serious deficits in his past. The nature of obsessions and compulsions are scary because they don't really make sense to the non-obsessive, non-compulsive person. The repetition and the need for porno can be rationalized——usually the rationalization comes from him, saying things like, "You are not giving me enough" or "This is just my type of entertainment and it's innocent."

These compulsions and obsessions can be worrisome. You might be asking yourself, "Why does he need this so often?" And that is a good question. Pornography can be a form of sexual acting out without having to take the risks——and be vulnerable——in the actual experience. It might just be some innocent fun or it might be an addiction and a substitution due to fears about doing the real thing.

An important part of all this is how uncomfortable you feel with it. If you feel threatened, you need to locate what's disturbing you. You can also try talking with your boyfriend, to get a real sense of what the lure is for him. Constant sexual excitement can be a defense against depression.

And you need to ask yourself, as honestly as you can, what am I really feeling about this? Does it disgust me? Is it too much and too often? In truth, we all have a great interest in sex, but how comfortable are you with this form of behavior? You need to trust what I call "the yuck factor," which can range from mildly uncomfortable to total nausea.

Don't deny what you are feeling!

You can trust yourself if you feel that pornography has taken over a person's consciousness, and if it feels "yucky" to you. Trust the yuck factor.

It's probably important to distinguish between pornography "lite"——which is more voyeuristic and harmless—— and high-calorie porn, which has more of a dangerous charge.

It recently came to my attention that someone I know has a terrible pornography addiction. He is very reckless and has captured his explorations on video and photographs that associate him with his professional life. It feels excessive and frightening to me. While I don't want to pass judgment on what consenting adults choose to do, I will say that if my husband expressed an interest in any of this, it would make me very uncomfortable and I would probably end up leaving the relationship. For me, there is a big difference between dressing up like a wayward milk maiden and using power tools as sex toys. One is playful and the other is just scary!

rationalization

You have said that white lies run the world and it would seem that rationalization would be "the process behind the process." Does rationalization provide the gusto for the white lies that we tell ourselves when we are faced with romantic disappointment?

The rationalization process is essentially an attempt to create a sense of logic for ourselves about doing something that we are really against doing. Rationalization is a way of justifying something by ignoring what we *know* to be true. Again, my friend Hannah's story is illustrative of this process. When she and her then fiancé left a concert hall one night, they discovered her future mother-in-law waiting outside with a cake that she had baked for her. Now there was no special occasion for the cake or any reason for the future mother-in-law to wait outside. Hannah was furious and felt like she was being stalked, and of course there was no response from the future ex-husband. She told him that this was awful and frightening, and that his mother had no boundaries. But he was the only son of his widowed mother, so he felt compelled to take her side. Eventually, after they married, Hannah rationalized that he would be able to take care of this situation and respect her feelings, which of course he never could do.

I guess it is part of my own process to feel alarmed, then analytical, then judgmental, then get into full-blown rationalization. Rationalization can keep us in a relationship long enough to find out why it is a terrible relationship and one that should be terminated. Would you agree?

This "R" word does keep coming up! We are talking about exchanges in the first few meetings when your brain is coming up with a lot of rationalizations for what you are hearing or what he is doing, and this is when your inner alarm clock is on "silent mode." Remember, rationalization is basically finding reasons to ignore something that you've already been alerted to—something that doesn't fit or that bothers you.

rationalization

A friend was once on a date with someone who, when introducing her, did not say, "Please say hello to my new friend Elizabeth." Instead, he'd say loudly, "This is Elizabeth. She's written two books and has a radio show." In other words, he recited her resume, without her permission, as a way to show off. What's important to realize is that he needed to do that to make himself feel better, to amp up his own self-esteem. Her rationalization process was as follows: her inner alarm said "this is disgusting." Then she thought, "Okay, nobody's perfect. I'm older now and I can't be so picky. Everybody has faults. There are other good things about him that I like." This is a very typical way we move into rationalization instead of embracing our feelings. We don't go near our feelings because they contain the seeds of truth about the matter. Rationalizing is like a big umbrella in a torrential storm. It keeps you from getting completely drenched at first, then the power of the wind and rain eventually blows it away, leaving you cold and soaked to the skin.

Look, the major difference between a fatal and non-fatal flaw is this: once something jumps out at you, the decisive issue is, does he care about the impact he's having on you? If he dismisses it, then that behavior is absolutely predictive of future results. He's your future ex-husband.

My friend, Rachel, is caught up in the rationalization process in a rather alarming way. I don't think there is anything that her boyfriend Seth can do that would cause her to say "enough." In fact, I recently told her that I could imagine him burning down their house and killing their dog, and she would find a way to be okay with it. I can just hear her saying, "While it was terribly impulsive I fully understand why Seth did what he did. Our house has dropped dramatically in value, he wanted central air conditioning, and he was sick of smelling the moldy basement."

Another friend is similarly entrenched in his rationalization process. Roman began dating a woman with the following profile: she was 15 years younger than he was, had experienced substance abuse issues, had been married at a very young age to an abusive older man, was bipolar, and had a host of other troubling issues. Of course there is an asterisk to everything and along with all of these blatant red flags were these facts: Camilla was attractive, had a great body, travelled the world, spoke French, and had studied classical ballet. When they started dating it became apparent that my friendship with Roman was in some way an irritant for Camilla. Every time that my husband and I met up with Roman for an evening, his cell phone would inevitably ring and it would be her. Roman would have to get into a long discourse about where he was and what he was doing and what time he would be home. He spent the next four years taking care of her while struggling to take care of himself. In the midst of all of this Camilla was invited to perform in Europe where she spent about six weeks on the road. She returned to New York and told Roman that she was in love and having an affair with a dancer and would soon be moving to Paris to live with him. Over the next two weeks she systematically burned every personal and professional bridge that she had cultivated. Finally she hit the wall and crashed when she realized that she had been used by this man and was now being discarded as he moved on to a new ingénue.

A month or so after this went down Roman and Camilla reconciled and were determined to leave New York and start a new life where his family lived and where they would have access to a support system of some kind. So they moved in with his parents in July and spent a lot of time at the beach, partying at bars, not working, and accumulating debt. She would sleep until early afternoon while he defended her lethargy to his parents, stressing the energy-depleting effects of her various medications. After eight months, Roman left for a few days to visit a friend who had been in a bad car accident. When he returned, he found out that Camilla had been seeing someone else, deliberately letting his family know about the transgression, and was completely unapologetic for her actions. To make matters worse, the person with whom she was having this affair was someone whose idea of a good time was to get a six pack and watch wrestling on cable TV. He did not speak French and probably never heard of Nijinsky and the Ballet Russe.

Here is a very stark example of how rationalization short circuits our ability to get in touch with our anger and instead allows us to feel wistful. Wistfulness is not the best response to an infidelity, but it is often the reaction of people who are terrified of being abandoned and have a history with betrayal.

Roman was obviously crushed by this loss. He said that he had dreams of starting anew with her and having a family. As he shared all of this with me I was thinking, "Hadn't Camilla provided enough information for him to run for his life and get as far away as possible?" Of course she did—over and over again. For several years, Roman held up the umbrella of rationalization to keep from getting rained on and now he was drowning in a tidal flood. Even after learning more about her aberrant behavior, he continued to feel sad and defeated, rather than experiencing a sense of relief.

I relate this story because it illustrates two very important processes: rationalization, along with identification with the damaged person, which in my opinion, feeds the sense of loss and makes it all the harder to disengage and move on with your life. His wistfulness was based on an inaccurate projection, like a mirage in the desert. There was never really a waterfall— only sand. Lots of it.

If you look beyond the extreme nature of the details, it was very similar to what I experienced with Arthur. I had the files before I moved in, and disregarded their contents.

Before Arthur, I had an even more intense experience of this process with Jake, whose wife had died only months before we started dating. As previously stated, the physical attraction was intense and a lot of florid letters and poetry went back and forth through the mail. When I wanted to know where we were at, or rather confirmation of where I assumed where we were at, he pulled back——dramatically. For Jake, the passion and the poetry had nothing to do with partnership. I rationalized that he felt guilty and that he had to create distance to cope with the grief he felt over his wife's death alongside the passion he felt for me. He once said, "You've rejuvenated my soul." How else was I supposed to hear that, other than, "This is a connection that I see going the distance"? Instead, I should have heard it as, "I love the intensity of our time together——but I need to get back in time for my tennis date at the country club." It was too painful for me to address things so starkly, so I rationalized everything that made me feel bad, and exaggerated everything that made me feel good.

religion

Is being religious stabilizing to the growth of a relationship? How important is it that two people share the same religion?

Religion also belongs in the category of "fit." It is usually a fit around our belief systems. A fundamentalist and an atheist don't fit very well together. Devoutness requires a certain intellectual and physical commitment; it's based on faith. That's why you can't argue religion. It has nothing to do with science or logic. It is ephemeral, and does not exist with proofs or disproofs.

Now, if you and your partner have different faiths, the central issue is whether you respect your differences. That takes great strength of character. If there is a way to find middle ground, that's wonderful, but that doesn't usually happen with two people of different faiths. A Jewish friend of mine had a daughter who was marrying a Catholic. The daughter did not choose to convert, but the wedding was going to be in a Catholic church. My friend found this unbearable, and it wasn't until the last minute that she decided to go to the wedding. The groom knew about this, and what emerged was a natural alienation. It was very hard to bridge these differences.

I think the issue is in being able to talk this out honestly, because this is an overlap with core needs and fit. If it's a core need for you to be identified with your religious faith, you have to listen to that.

If your partner practices an Orthodox religion, you have to be aware that this entails rigid organization of one's life——sex, food, clothes——and this has to be discussed with absolute honesty. But the biggest discussion is the one you have to have with yourself.

Do you think an Orthodox religion makes the commitment of marriage any easier?

Religious people have the same problems as everyone else, and it is not apparent how religion helps them solve their problems. In fact, it often can repress the problems, especially when people use religion to not have to deal with personal differences. They didn't have religion issues, but interpersonal ones that religion can't control.

This is the one area, generally speaking, where my husband and I do not agree. He is vehemently against organized religion, while it is of great interest to me, even though I am not a religious person per se. However, he will fully admit that had we had our own children, he would have been perfectly fine with them being raised Jewish, and would have happily driven them to Hebrew school.

If you are dating someone who is very religious, and he feels that his path is the only righteous one, ask yourself if he is hiding behind this worldview and if he is using it as defense against a bevy of unprocessed issues. If that's the case, you just have to decide if this is not obstructive to you getting your needs met by him.

There's that great saying, "Those who think they know, don't know. Those who think that they don't know, know." The institutionalization of belief makes me uncomfortable.

safety

When you speak of the importance of feeling safe, do you mean physical safety or emotional safety?

There are two kinds of safety issues: physical and psychological. If you have issues and concerns that your relationship isn't going to be physically safe, don't wait until you have to get an order of protection——GET OUT NOW! Nothing can justify the threat of violent behavior or actual violent behavior. Just get out.

Psychological safety itself really has to do with feeling safe with someone two different ways. One way is predictability. Example: You know how your boyfriend will act or react, and you're comfortable with it.

The second, bigger issue is, "Can I be who I really am with this person?" For instance, when I was young I had a great sense of humor that I believed wasn't okay to show to men. Today in my relationships, I no longer hold back a vital part of my irreverent self. Not that I have to demonstrate it all the time, but I want to feel safe that when my humor and irreverence emerge, they will find an understanding and a respected place with my partner. Psychological safety is really about not having to suppress important parts of yourself, and being able to trust that these aspects of you will be respected and/or tolerated by a partner. It doesn't mean a partner has to like all the parts of you, but there is a fundamental understanding that you both can be who you are in this relationship and not have to monitor thoughts, feelings, and emotions in order to maintain a certain image. If you do have to maintain an image, then you cannot be "safe," because so much energy needs to be invested in maintaining the image indefinitely, so the truth won't emerge.

I am very familiar with both sides of the safety issue. For a long time I was with someone I did not feel safe with, and that often felt exciting and edgy. When you're on a roller coaster you may not feel completely safe, and it is exciting for some and terrifying for others. When I was speaking to a close friend once about a mutual friend who has never been in a relationship, she said that "for Martha to be able to be comfortable with a man, she would have to be stuck in an elevator with him for three days straight. Maybe then she'd feel safe." While that's a bit of an exaggeration, it does reveal a very powerful truth: that so many of us simply cannot feel safe very easily and that it takes an extraordinary set of circumstances for us to be comfortable with being vulnerable.

sex

I have always found that sex interferes with good judgement. The men with whom I shared the greatest passion were ultimately not potential partners. I could never reconcile this with everything we are shown about love and romance——by books, movies, music, all of our cultural touchstones. How important is sex as a predictor of a good relationship?

You know you are in trouble if on the first couple of dates the man lets you know how important sex is to him. That's code for "you better do what I like in bed." It's a set-up for having sex *his* way, and the amount of it *he* wants. Another signal in that direction is kinky talk from the beginning, when you really don't know each other. The emphasis is more on his sex drive than on getting to know you. And certainly any verbal history of his sex life is deadly. Don't even try a second date.

Q What about the physical side, the sexual responsiveness, or in some case, non-responsiveness?

A When the guy is not responsive to being pleasured, it raises serious questions about possible anxiety and fear of his sexuality and potential for intimacy. There needs to eventually be mutuality in sex. Relationships mean you *and* me, not you *or* me. That represents certain mutuality at the heart of the relationship. If the sex only goes in one direction, it raises serious questions about his sexual blocks. Your pleasure will begin to decrease quickly because of the one-sidedness. No matter how you try to change it, sex is an interactive behavior.

Q What about passionate, uninhibited sex?

Uninhibited sex is a good sign, depending on the appropriateness. Good relationships are like plants: they need healthy ground. Sexual relationships on the whole benefit from creating the ground of knowing somebody—familiarity and growing closeness. That is, creating an appropriate and nurturing environment for the plant that is the relationship. Having sex too quickly to please him rather than to please the two of you is a way of flooding the plant, lifting its roots from the ground, and thus endangering its life.

We're wired for sexual attraction. Infatuation is important, but keep in mind the building and fertilizing of the ground first. Then you will have healthy and nutritious soil for your budding relationship.

Everyone is wired differently, so all of this is contextual. I honestly don't think it is possible to be in a longstanding relationship that is safe and happy, and expect to have serially mind-blowing sex. My husband has coined an expression that he refers to as "the whiff." This is where the initial days, weeks, and months of the relationship are wrapped in superlatives.

Age also figures into things here. When we are in our 20s and 30s, sex is very different than it is when we are in our 40s, 50s, and 60s. As we get older, other things come into our lives that give it depth and richness, that often displace the urgency that once accompanied having sex. I consider myself very lucky to have had "the whiff" and the passion that went with it. However, I am even luckier to be happily married to someone with whom reading in bed or watching *Apocalypse Now* for the umpteenth time is just as enjoyable. A friend said it best——"When it's there, it's 10% of the relationship. When it's not there, it's 90%." While midlife hormonal changes have definitely affected my libido, it is very important for me to indulge in snuggling and everything else that goes with real intimacy, which is much broader than sex.

soul-mate-at-first-sight phenomenon

I know that this can sound so ethereal and cinematic, but don't we all have a soul mate somewhere, or at least hope that we do? Sometimes you do have a profound "hit" upon meeting someone, which feels like the deepest connection imaginable. Is that totally invalid?

I think this phenomenon is about really impulsive behavior being rationalized in the name of something spiritual. A central issue within narcissism is "what I need from somebody else so I'll feel related to and good about myself." One of the important things for a healthy sense of self is to have the "twinship" aspect——somebody who understands us and likes us. The use of spirituality is often a cover for deep-seated impulsiveness and a quick way to actually meet the need for the relationship.

soul-mate-at-first-sight phenomenon

Are you saying you cannot have a real relationship with someone you believe is your soul mate?

What often happens in the first stage of a relationship is infatuation, but it is articulated as a "soul connection." When you go that high and go so quickly, you're destined for disappointment when the infatuation dies and you're dealing with the real person in complex situations. The need for fusion——I'm you and you're me——is a very narcissistic quality and can be a defense against a feeling of abandonment. The need for fusion and identity is often found in cults and very extreme fundamentalist religions. It's very enticing, and it might be true for a while, but then the differences begin to show up. If and when I start to be more me and less fusion-oriented, self-needs emerge, and the other person receives it as some kind of rejection. Or their self-needs begin to emerge, and then you start to look like less of a soul mate. People think soul mates have no place for conflict, so you're disqualified upon differentiation!

To maintain the "soul" connection, all of your needs have to be subsumed within or consumed by the soul mate idealization. Another aspect is the idealization itself. When that happens, the idealizations tend to polarize between somebody who is perfect and marvelous, and someone who is not.

If you can stay in the perfect-and-marvelous zone, then things will be good for a while. But when differences emerge, and they will, there's a danger of moving to the other pole, which means you're a jerk. You make the stakes very high in order to maintain the soul mate status, and no middle ground is allowed. Soul mate romances often end in disappointment or with you having to squelch aspects of yourself.

Isn't idealization necessary?

Yes, but there is a difference between infatuation and the soul mate thing. And if you look at the divorce rate, which is over 50%, then you have to see that a lot of people got disappointed. Again, in earlier times marriage was not necessarily about love, but about business. The romantic idea, as we know it today, is relatively new. This is a landmark time for women in having the opportunity to acquire more money, more power, and thus, more choice. This has changed the whole functional spectrum of long-term mating.

We tend to live primarily in cities, and community is disappearing or has already disappeared. People are isolated in both the suburbs and city apartments. I think there are deep needs for connectedness that are not being played out as in our past: in our caves, tribes, villages, etc. The hunger for that kind of attachment is also connected to the concept of the soul mate: "Somewhere in this great universe there is a special person for me, who will know me the second he meets me." It's not only a fantasy, but verges on delusion. It has created expectations that are impossible to be met. If you have an experience that is a little less than the soul mate experience, you might be giving up other important connections that you've made. The soul mate, who eventually might become a roommate, is probably later on in danger of becoming your future ex-husband.

Would you agree that there is currently an epidemic need for idealization?

Yes. The idealization of celebrities in our lives is absurd. It's a way of passively *becoming* a celebrity, of walking in their shoes and feeling special. We all want to feel special. We need to look at what's happened to us causing this need for idealization, for it to fill us so much.

Obviously, the media have taken over. We're seeing people all the time in all these idealized ways, in overblown circumstances. That's one of the major things behind eating disorders——unrealistic images shoved down people's throats. People today tend to mix their own realities with what they think are celebrity/media realities, which really are primarily just images.

I have experienced soul-mate-at-first-sight phenomenon many times and it really encapsulates "the whiff" and its intoxicating properties. It is narcissism, projection, and over-rationalization all in one package. My relationship with Jake was very much of this genetic disposition. For me there was an absolute need for fusion, and for him, a very pronounced desire to be seen as a Renaissance man. Several weeks after we met, he sent me a letter and a poem. I was just coming out of my decade-long codependent relationship with David. The wallop and "whiff" of this new person was overwhelming, and I reacted very impulsively in many ways. I felt that I had to match his "specialness" and confirm our soul-mate-ness by providing an even stronger letter and poem. I remember actually willing myself to write; an inner voice saying, "You better get good——fast!" Because of my family history, I am someone with very significant abandonment issues, which has cultivated a pronounced need to fuse, often inappropriately. Predictably, when my needs started to emerge, when I wanted to move beyond the erotic engagement, then all of a sudden the fairy dust dissipated. I felt rejected when he was fine making plans without me. Once disagreement or incongruity emerged, I was disqualified upon differentiation.

trust

This is such a central issue. Without trust, there can essentially be no relationship. But I find myself asking, "Is trust a fluid kind of thing?" In some situations my trust is absolute. In others, it wavers. Is that really acceptable?

There are circumstances that mold experience. We are talking about psychological trust. In other words, I'm not really worried that my boyfriend is going to steal my jewelry. This type of trust emerges from a few different factors, the main one being predictability. An example: even if I can predict that my boyfriend will be a schmuck every Friday night, I can still feel safe with him.

It's like our relationship with our mother: we knew what would make her angry and what would get us hugs, so we trusted her psychologically. The same thing with friends. We have friends we are sure of and friends we are not. It doesn't matter if you're a jerk, but if I can *predict* when you are going to act like a jerk, I can feel safe with you. Predictability is paramount to trust. That comes from infancy. Trust is also about not having to monitor ourselves.

A shift in behavior causes an alert. If the shift continues, there is no question that the amount of anxiety and distrust will rise. Consistency is a significant part of psychological trust, which is the kind we're interested in. Adultery shatters the base of the trust because it is a profound violation of predictability and consistency. It is almost a cliché to say that once that trust has been destroyed, it's hard to put Humpty Dumpty together again. And there's a fine line between abuse and normal behaviors: If you catch your husband looking in your checkbook, that can be a warning sign. Is he impinging on your trust? Is this a trust breakdown? It could be a cry for help; that your relationship is in trouble.

I know a woman who met a man who worked in her office——who also had an 18-month-old child and a pregnant wife——and she fell in love with him. They had a mad affair and eventually he left his wife and proposed to her. Before she married him, in one clear moment, she said, "If he did it to her, he can do it to me," but she still rationalized and married him. Eight years later he left her with two children, overnight, just like that. She ignored her inner voice. You have to respect your inner voice.

Why is it that so often we don't listen to our inner voice? My husband likes to say that we "always know what the shot is" and he is right. I remember being with Jake for New Year's Eve. Things had been shaky and it was clear that this would be our last time together. On New Year's Day he left the house to go for a quick run. Filled with despair and a compulsion to understand his rejection, I noticed his journal lying on the coffee table. In a moment of unbridled anxiety, I opened it, and read a passage that——predictably——deeply hurt my feelings. His unavailability only fired up my not trusting him, which was amplified by my belief that I would never find someone as appealing and as interesting as him again. I did not trust that I could create a better situation. If I did, I never would have read his journal. As an aside, I was never able to fall asleep whenever we spent the night together. I would literally be up the entire evening and early morning, feeling over-stimulated, under-appreciated, and anticipating the next opportunity for synthetic fusion.

I trust my husband absolutely, and I am not only referring to marital fidelity. I trust that he has learned from his own experiences, that he knows right from wrong, that he knows who is on his team, and most important, that he knows that our relationship, our love, represents all of the good that exists within each of us. To not respect that truth would be the worst violation of trust, and neither of us is getting on that bus.

asking questions we are afraid to ask

I have dated many potential future ex-husbands, but fortunately have never married any of them!

Despite my sadness and bemoaning following the dissolution of each relationship, I knew deep down that the man-of-the-moment was not the right one for me to think about marrying. There was always something I was busy rationalizing, defending, or denying——a huge red flag that something was not right.

After I filed a complete report of every negative exchange, a friend would often ask, "Deb, when you take the milk out of the refrigerator and it smells sour, do you put it back in?" I think that women in general have a phenomenal ability to remember each and every detail of any type of information exchanged with their partner. As someone with many relationship transcripts to refer to in my files, I find it fascinating that so many behaviors, remarks, and actions went unnoticed and did not trigger a more appropriate response on my part.

I hope you will get many ideas, suggestions, and answers from this book. But the most important thing that you can take away with you is that you can start asking some of these questions and observe how you respond to and act on the answers you eventually get.

I have not ceased to be amazed by the evolution of the relationship with my husband. He has never been late for a date or an appointment, he has never lied, and he actually listens to what I say. In short, he shows up, is not a raging narcissist, and never gives me any material for endless analytical sessions with my friends. He is a "fit."

I believe the most important aspect of our history is that we were friends first. There was not the soul-mate-at-first-sight phenomenon. We hung out with each other and our friends and realized just how much we enjoyed each other's company. Our unconscious courtship was conducted over six months of Scrabble® games and watching movies.

While my superstitious nature urges me not to be presumptive, I take great joy and comfort that I can look forward to repeated viewings of *I, Claudius*, *The Godfather*, and *Some Like it Hot*——the fruits of genuine and healthy fusion.

about the author

Debra Weiner is a writer who lives in Montclair, New Jersey, with her husband and two cats. She is presently working on a novel, and a poetry manuscript. Debra's favorite place in the world is Rome, where she hopes to continue her writing on the Aventine hill.

www.ingramcontent.com/pod-product-compliance
Lightning Source LLC
LaVergne TN
LVHW051839080426
835512LV00018B/2970